THE KING LEAR EXPERIENCE

THE KING LEAR EXPERIENCE

With Complete Text by

WILLIAM SHAKESPEARE

Edited and Introduced by James A. Epperson

Interpretive Drawings by Gobin Stair

BEACON PRESS   BOSTON

Beacon Press books are published under the auspices of
the Unitarian Universalist Association
Published simultaneously in hardcover and paperback editions
All rights reserved
Printed in the United States of America

(hardcover) 9 8 7 6 5 4 3 2 1

(paperback) 9 8 7 6 5 4 3 2 1

Library of Congress Cataloging in Publication Data

Shakespeare, William, 1564–1616.
    The King Lear experience.
    I. Epperson, James A.   II. Stair, Gobin.
III. Title.
PR2819.A2E6   1976   822.3′3   75–36040
ISBN 0–8070–6380–0
ISBN 0–8070–6381–9 (pbk.)

Contents

Reading KING LEAR

However much we may argue about its elusive meaning and infinite complexity, *King Lear* is generally regarded as Shakespeare's greatest play. Its profundity is universally recognized, yet no one has expressed precisely the nature of this profound drama in words that satisfy all. Although the play is disturbing, its disturbances create in us a thoughtful consideration of our humanity rather than a despairing or nihilistic judgment of man. The language is moving and powerful even as it is enigmatic. As an example of dramatic art, it poses virtually insurmountable problems for actors and directors, yet *King Lear* is produced almost annually and continues to attract those in the theatrical world who wish to test their skills and ambitions in this most rewarding play.

Familiarity with the play paradoxically increases its value as well as our respect for its unresolved and subtle ironies. Knowledge of *King Lear* does not result in complacent conclusions. Instead, such knowledge strengthens our understanding of ourselves and others, liberates us from the exigencies of our daily concerns, and thus enables us to contemplate and evaluate the actions of human beings, the motions of society, and the purposes of our lives.

This familiarity and knowledge is not easily attained. And while no one would deny the value of the effort, *King Lear* remains a difficult play in every respect. It demands actors of almost superhuman range and power. It is directed to a mature, thoughtful audience. Since most of us initially encounter the play as readers, we are aware of the strains it puts on our concentration and experience. Yet if we persevere, the drama yields its wisdom.

Some of the obstacles that stand between us and that wisdom are to be found not in *King Lear* but in the fact and form of its greatness. In other words, we know *of* Shakespeare's famous drama before we actually experience the force of its tragedy; and many of us *read* the play before we see and hear it enacted on the stage.

These facts necessarily influence the way we approach *King Lear* and, indeed, any of the great works of art which are so well known as to be preceded by their reputations. Whether created two or five centuries ago, the music of Bach, the sculpture of Michelangelo, or the plays of Shakespeare are enthusiastically admired in the present. Since we have been told of the capacity of these works to illuminate our understanding and enrich our lives, we possess a pre-sense of great art before we experience its presence. Such enduring reputation attracts us and testifies to the universal and virtually eternal value of those rare creations of man that transcend space, time, and cultural change.

Yet the very esteem with which, say, Shakespeare's plays are regarded causes problems. Because we have been told that *King Lear* is a great play, we approach it with reverence and some uncertainty. Aware of its exalted stature, and of the learned authorities who have certified its profundity, we enter its presence as humble petitioners, hoping to sound, if only partially, some of the deeps the play contains. We put aside hopes of entertainment even as we arouse the intellect for the effort of understanding we believe we must make. Consequently, we go to the theater to see *King Lear*, or pick up the text, with feelings of apprehension. Will we be worthy of the assured and sanctified greatness of the play? Will it live up to our expectations? Having these questions—and they are hard to ignore —we are likely to regard *King Lear* as an arduous test, both of our sensitivity and intelligence and of our predispositions. Thus when we initially come to the play, both we and it are at a disadvantage. We fear that our response will be inadequate; the play suffers because it seldom matches our anticipation.

Despite these uncertainties, *King Lear* and other magnificent works of art remain vital. Each generation discovers and then perpetuates their vitality and penetrating significance. The process of discovery, however, requires effort and sometimes knowledge. For example, one is struck immediately by the serene beauty of Michelangelo's statue of David, but the complexity of the figure becomes apparent only after contemplation: the masterful depiction of courage, controlled power, heroic confidence, and youthful beauty—all are interfused in our minds with the biblical narrative of David slaying the giant Goliath. The statue becomes dramatic. We see David at a moment of intense psychological concentration, not after his victory, but just before the struggle, as he looks upon his fearsome adversary. Being familiar with the story, we know he shall triumph. But for David, the outcome is in doubt; yet his attitude is one of vigorous, intelligent resolution. The psychological drama of the moment, presented so economically by the genius of Michelangelo, is unforgettable.

The process of contemplation leading to recognition and illumination is the same with *King Lear*. Nevertheless, there are differences. David is there, in Florence, to be seen; it is a visual and static work of art, neither speaking nor moving. It is meant to be looked at, and nothing comes between the object and the gaze. Independent and self-contained, the statue needs only space to stand in. *King Lear*, on the other hand, is a play meant to be enacted for an audience. It thus requires actors and a stage. Reading the play is like seeing only a photograph of Michelangelo's David; yet most of us are introduced to *King Lear* by means of a text which we read and then, perhaps, study. We study the language, the structure, characterization, and sometimes the sources, the transmission of the text, or the commentaries of those who have themselves studied and written about the play—or we hear our teachers read lectures.

To be sure, these are valuable ways of coming to know a dramatic work of art. And reading *King Lear* can be a more satisfactory experience than sitting through an inept and embarrassing performance. The reader can imagine a production of his own that exists somewhere between the artifice of the stage and the reality of the world. A text also allows us to re-read certain passages, linger over fine speeches, or compare separate parts. The action that goes by so swiftly on the stage is frozen in the script and thus susceptible to the probing and subtle analysis of the critic and scholar. Finally, a mass-produced printed text makes the play widely available and frees us from a dependency on the theater. To discover *King Lear* we are not obliged to wait for a local company to produce the play; nor do we need to travel to New York or London (where *King Lear* has been staged almost every season for the past fifteen years). We can enter the thunderous and tragic world that Shakespeare created simply by opening the book whenever we choose and wherever we are.

Despite these advantages—and there are others—reading a play does a disservice to the design and form of a drama. *King Lear* is more than words; it is a spectacle that unfolds and develops before our eyes. When we are in the theater the action is dynamic, immediate, and continuous, seemingly with a life of its own. Yet, as any experienced actor will testify, the audience contributes to that life with its presence and response. Drama is a communal act. And simply being in a theater, traveling there, buying a ticket, taking a seat, then feeling hopeful anticipation as the play begins, heightens the experience, detaches it from our everyday routine. We then find ourselves willingly subject to the mind and imagination of another, in this case Shakespeare, regarded not only as the greatest dramatist in English but also as one of the supreme half-dozen literary artists in the history of mankind.

However, when we see a play like *King Lear* for the first time, certain words and perhaps entire speeches may not be clear. We are then reminded that Shakespeare wrote nearly four hundred years ago, using words that have either dropped from our vocabulary or changed meaning. We cannot stop the actor and ask him to define an archaic word or unscramble the syntax of a speech. Instead, we attend and, by attending, understand the general meaning of the action, even as we remain ignorant of details. Furthermore, some of the ideas and relationships in the play are as unknown to us as some of the words. To take only one example, what are we to make of the idea of monarchy, a system of government that, virtually universal in Shakespeare's time, has practically disappeared in the twentieth century? We cannot expect an explanation of the nature of monarchy in the sixteenth century to interrupt the action of the play. We simply try to surmise what it was like to have a ruler of the power of King Lear, then trust in the coherence of the play to make sense of a political system we can only imagine.

Several excellent editions of *King Lear* solve these problems by offering the reader notes and commentary. These devices, however, useful as they are to students and scholars, frequently intimidate the reader. Notes, glosses, and learned explanations also tend to interrupt the play's relentless and purposeful development, and thus interfere with the reader's total concentration on, and submission to, the action. Even while recognizing their value, most readers have been daunted or distracted by pages of commentary and thickets of finely printed footnotes.

The Beacon Press edition of *King Lear* is an experiment, the presentation of a text designed to be *seen* as well as *read*. Using the techniques of modern book production, the editors have sought to imitate (not copy) some of the visual and psychological effects one experiences in the theater. Some liberties have been taken with the customary arrangement of the lines (although the text is complete, and follows in general the readings of modern textual editions of the play). As in the theater, there are no footnotes, and the language is largely presented as prose. An "Afterword," for those who wish to know more about the drama, contains some comments on Shakespeare's language, together with some brief paragraphs on the text of *King Lear* and on some recent critical discussions of the play.

What follows is a rationale for the experiment and an interpretation of *King Lear* that serves as a guide for this reader's edition. Our intention is to make more accessible the play's power and intensity, to emphasize its majestic and eternal relevance by means of a page bearing both words and images. This combination of verbal and visual information conveys to the reader clearer expressions of dramatic relationships and conflicts, more of the subtleties of tone and nuance, than are normally found in the traditional editions of *King Lear.*

It is always useful to begin with the obvious. *King Lear* was not written to be read; it was written to be heard. The words of the play were copied out so that actors could speak them aloud to an audience. The characters, so tersely designated on the page by a mere name, are meant to speak and move upon a stage, to possess the several characteristics of any human being: a face, a tone of voice, a general appearance, appropriate clothing, youth or age, beauty or ugliness, a relationship to others, and a personal history. Thus the name "Cordelia" printed on the page tells us almost nothing of the woman we are meant to see and hear. The name "Albany" does not begin to suggest the complex figure of husband, ruler, son-in-law, and troubled avenger we meet in the course of the drama. From such obvious comparisons we can start to understand the essential artificiality of reading, as opposed to attending, a play in the theater, that is, experiencing a dramatic work as intended by its author.

The major difference, of course, is that in the theater we *see* and *hear* the characters. We watch King Lear as he divides his kingdom among his daughters, and we see how the daughters, their suitors, Kent, and the courtiers *react* to the King's decisions. We see the expressions on their faces, the gestures they make with their hands and bodies, the positions they take relative to one another. And all of these sights are loaded with information that cannot be delivered solely by words on the page. Without their telling us, we notice and record their ages, their physical size, and even their position in society. From the costume of a character we can determine whether he is rich or poor, a soldier or a civilian, a priest or a judge, a king or a fool.

In the theater we hear the rage and sorrow of King Lear in the way he speaks as well as in the words he uses. The nuance, inflection, and emphasis with which a skilled actor delivers his lines convey information not apparent in the printed text. For example, when King Lear turns to Cordelia and asks her what she can say as a measure of her love for him, she utters only one word: "Nothing." This solitary word, of course, has a powerful effect on the King and all of the succeeding action. It is one of the hinges upon which the drama turns. But how should this significant word be spoken? What should the audience hear when Cordelia gives that startling answer? A trained and talented actress could speak in tones that would hint at Cordelia's dilemma: a reluctance to express her love in terms of dishonest exaggeration, yet a desire to admit (with perhaps too much precision) that she loves her father according to her bond, "no more nor less."

We hear sounds that add information and atmospheric density to particular scenes: trumpets heralding the entry of a king, the clash of weapons during battle, the cacophony of the wind and rain and thunder. These and many other sights and sounds are provided for the theatergoer, but the reader of *King Lear* is denied these appeals to eye and ear. To the reader, the words are silent, the characters motionless.

Despite such liabilities, despite the absence of the sights and sounds of the stage, many readers manage to overcome the limitations of the page. They "see" the characters move with the "mind's eye." They hear the voices and sounds of the play with the mind's ear. In other words, they imagine the play enacted, as it were, in the theater of the mind.

This ability to imagine the action of a play is perhaps a learned skill, although some people seem to learn it without much effort. Others, especially those who never or infrequently go to the theater, have difficulty meeting the demands that the printed text puts on the imagination. And a play read from a book does place astonishing burdens on us. We must literally create the characters and their actions, imagining their appearance, age, voices, dress, and gestures.

Of course, the text assists our imagination with some necessary information. In the case of King Lear, for example, we know that he is old when he tells the court (and us) that he wishes "To shake all cares and business" from his life and "Unburdened crawl toward death." Later we learn that his age is "fourscore and upward." We also learn that he has daughters, loyal servants, and a rash and imperious temper. From these facts and others we can deduce his general personality and appearance. But what, specifically, is he wearing? We can imagine the voice and gestures of an old man, but what *kind* of voice, and what *manner* of gesture?

The text also helps us imagine the settings of particular scenes. We know that Lear is out in a fierce and terrible storm because the characters describe the storm in precisely those terms. Or at one point, when Lear awakens from his sleep, we imagine the sounds of music because the Doctor calls out, "Louder the music there!" Such details enliven even as they control our mind's eye and ear. Sometimes the characters will describe specific gestures made by themselves or others. For example, we can easily imagine Lear tearing at his clothes when, after defining "unaccommodated man" as a "poor, bare, forked animal," he says, "Off, off, you lendings! Come; unbutton here."

Finally, the most obvious helps to the reader are the stage directions provided by the author or his editors. Some playwrights, like George Bernard Shaw, include whole paragraphs of detailed stage and acting directions in their plays, while the laconic directions in Shakespeare's plays—"Enter Lear in a chair carried by Servants" is one of the longest in the play—help the reader (and director) only insofar as they indicate entrances and exits of particular characters. As far as we know, Shakespeare did not write all the stage directions into his plays, probably because the author, himself an actor and member of the company, orally directed the players as they rehearsed. Many of the directions that do appear in Shakespeare's plays were most likely (and in some cases certainly) inserted by his first and subsequent editors.

This difference of seeing and hearing rather than reading a play may be illustrated by one final, but telling, example. While reading a play we occasionally get the characters mixed up, especially if they are of about the same age, sex, and class. The problem is compounded if the characters are, say, brothers having several similar traits. (Such confusion is a source of comedy, as Shakespeare knew when he borrowed from Plautus the device of twins as the central comic mixup of the *Comedy of Errors*.) Such a problem occurs in *King Lear*. The Earl of Gloucester has two sons, Edmund and Edgar, names roughly alike in spelling and appearance on the page. Edmund, however, is a bastard son and disloyal. Edgar is the lawful son and loyal. Yet while reading a speech of Edmund's we may have to stop and go backward in the text to remind ourselves of the distinction between the brothers. This confusion disappears in a stage production, for we easily distinguish Edmund from Edgar by his characteristic voice, stature, carriage, dress, and manner. In short, characters are effortlessly identified by sight and sound.

Thus a reader of a play stands in a severely limited relationship to the total possible experience of dramatic art. He is in the position of one who arrives at the theater only to find that the production has been struck, the sets dismantled, the costumes packed away, the actors scattered, and the auditorium dark and empty. All that remains is the script, the bare record of the words spoken by the characters. If he is interested in the play, he must reconstruct from the text and with his imagination the production that has disappeared.

This edition of *King Lear* is designed to assist the reader with that task. It attempts to fill the gap between witnessing a full-blown stage production and reading words on a page. Of course, a book cannot speak (although one can listen to a recording of a play while following the script), and a page cannot convey motion. But the page can show us things, appealing as it does directly to our vision. We read, obviously, with our eyes, and we can see informative objects on a page other than letters and words. It seems logical, then, that the techniques of book design and typography and the skills of the graphic artist can serve as a useful bridge between the printed and staged play. The images that appear on the following pages cannot reproduce a stage production exactly, but they can imitate certain visual details and therefore suggest significant interpretations of the action and the characters.

One who has developed the skill of reading a dramatic text reads as a director might review a script. But to stage a play, a good director must arrive at some total conception of the drama, a principle of coherence, selection, and emphasis with which to create a powerfully unified production. Uncertainty in the director's mind about the ultimate meaning of a play is likely to result in a confused, ineffective performance. Without this guiding conception, there is no way to determine and integrate the thousands of decisions the director must make as he prepares the play for the stage. Even such relatively minor details as the costumes of the characters, the colors to be used in the sets and lighting, or the props to be carried by the actors should contribute to what the director perceives as the play's central dramatic experience.

Once the director has discovered or formulated what that central experience is, he can begin to "dress" the production, cast the actors for the various roles, design the sets, determine the lighting, ascertain relationships, create emphasis, and direct the actors in their vocal and physical actions. In short, a good director and a skilled reader must arrive at an *interpretation* of the play.

It is false to think that the minute the word "interpretation" enters the discussion we are likely to fall into subjective confusion or universal contradiction. While it is true that there may be many interpretations of *King Lear*, it is also true that some interpretations are better than others because they are truer to the *facts* of the play. For instance, one fact is the death of Cordelia at the play's end. This undoubted event in *King Lear* was so repugnant to Nahum Tate, a seventeenth-century writer, that he rewrote the play with an ending in which Cordelia survives to marry Edgar. We may smile at Tate's evasion of the facts and the sentimental interpretation that emerged, but other less obvious evasions of twentieth-century directors and actors have resulted in similarly bizarre distortions of the facts Shakespeare put into his play. The following interpretation is, it is hoped, true to *King Lear*, and the remainder of this introduction argues its validity, then applies it to the typographical and graphic "staging" of the text itself.

When we sit in the audience of a play, we are at once detached and interested. We look in on the lives of the characters without their knowledge, and overhear and oversee their utterances and motions. As the play progresses, our interest deepens; we witness a conflict and anticipate with increasing curiosity its resolution. At the end of the performance we can usually recount what the play was about—what the conflict was and how it was resolved. We might be able to formulate words that approximate the central theme or basic proposition that generated the action.

What is *King Lear* about? What is its major concern? Asking such a simple question of such a complex drama raises some immediate problems. How can we sort out the most significant speeches and actions from the seemingly disparate yet related and ironic details of the play? Let us begin with the most obvious fact: the play is about two families, King Lear's and the Earl of Gloucester's. And insofar as it is about families, it is concerned with the conflict of generations, parents (in this case, fathers) and children in opposition. The parents have wealth, power, and authority. The children desire these, and some of them (Goneril, Regan, and Edmund) use deceit, flattery, and outright treachery to satisfy their desires.

In so acting, these children ignore or violate their "nature," the "bond" that ties parent and child together, the fundamental and biologically unbreakable relationship between the creators (parents) and the created (children). In this respect *King Lear* has been called "elemental," for it enacts one of the most primary, universal, and therefore elemental facts of man's nature: that all men and women have parents. Because of this fact, there is a bond between the parent and child, ostensibly a bond of love, but a bond sometimes regretted; then the bond becomes simply bondage.

This bond can be imperfect, resented, or misunderstood. Edmund is bound only biologically to his father and therefore, in Shakespeare's world, partially. Legally he is a bastard, illegitimate, and consequently "futureless" in regard to inheriting the patrimony of Gloucester. He must make his way *as if* there were no bond between him and his father. And Gloucester misunderstands or trivializes his bond with Edmund when he jokes about Edmund's conception and illegitimacy.

At the beginning of the play, when dividing up his kingdom, Lear places an unrealistic stress on the parent-child bond, thus treating his daughters *as if* they were in bondage, bound to flatter him like bond-slaves. Goneril and Regan, reacting in kind to Lear's unreal demands, exaggerate the true bond of filial love that Cordelia invokes, deceive their father with excess, and eventually violate their filial bond, driving Lear out into the storm and into madness.

The terrifying action of the play thus begins when Lear fails to see the limits of this natural bond between parent and child. Believing the flattery of Goneril and Regan, he is blind to the truth of Cordelia's bald assertion that she loves him according to her bond, "no more nor less." He also ignores another fundamental fact of human life: that the created (children) grow to become themselves potential creators (parents). Cordelia reminds Lear of this future alteration of the bonds of love—from filial to marital—when she says, "Haply, when I shall wed, / That lord whose hand must take my plight shall carry / Half my love with him, half my care and duty."

Lear is blind to another bond, that of loyalty (a form of love), based not on blood but on affection, friendship, and service, consequently a contractual and voluntary bond that can be broken. When Kent intercedes on behalf of Cordelia and enjoins the King to "see better" the true, though painfully blunt, sincerity of his youngest daughter's love, Lear furiously exiles Kent from the kingdom. The King on his side thus snaps the bonds of loyalty that have tied Kent to him. Even so, Kent maintains his loyalty by later serving Lear as the disguised Caius. However, before his exile and change of identity, Kent reminds Lear (and the audience) of the loving relationships that Kent believes give him the right, and even duty, to question the King's judgment of Cordelia. In his careful reply to the angry King, Kent describes a complex and multiple relationship to Lear that is at once familial and political, and therefore the source of a steadfast loyalty that is both personal and social. In Kent's eyes Lear is more than a king; he is,

"Royal Lear, whom I have ever honor'd as my king, loved as my father, as my master follow'd, as my great patron thought on in my prayers—"

In these words of Kent, whose bond exists outside the family, yet who describes Lear as king, father, master, and patron, and whose exemplary love of Lear remains steady even in the darkest times, we can begin to see that *King Lear* is about those broader relationships we call politics. Initially the concern is with the politics of the family; then the focus widens to concentrate on the politics of that greater family, a society or state. For as the play progresses, we see the main characters entangled in politics, those shifting relationships that, in the play as in life, are concerned with the aggressions of war, the acquisition of wealth, power, and prestige, attempts to promote order and harmony, and the gratification of desire. One side in the conflict (that represented by Goneril, Regan, Cornwall, and Edmund) establishes these political relationships and subsequent claims to power on illegitimate and unnatural grounds. These four break the filial and social bonds of love that Kent described, and then bind themselves one to another with fear and treachery. Their sovereignty is maintained, not with the love and respect and honor that Lear has created in Kent, but with the oppressive use of naked force, the twists and turns of conspiracy, and appeals to the appetites for sex, riches, or status.

The oppositions in *King Lear* may thus be stated as oppositions within the family (between the generations) and a larger opposition within that larger organization of men called a society. One group ignores or violates the "natural" bonds between parent and child, king and subject, master and servant. The other group willingly observes the constraints and obligations of those bonds. The two groups justify their actions with interpretations of that difficult, ambiguous, and—in *King Lear*—ubiquitous concept "Nature."

Throughout the play, characters define attitudes and events as "natural" or "unnatural" or as "monstrous." (A monster in Elizabethan English meant something out of nature, deviating from the norm. A misshapen creature, a two-headed calf or malformed child, was called a monster.) Edmund, who speaks for those who violate the bonds of nature observed by others, defines *his* nature and the life of man as a war of each against all. He will not be bound by the "plagues of custom," the distinctions within the society, or even the law. "Edmund the base," he confidently asserts, "shall top the legitimate" Edgar.

Others (primarily Cordelia, Kent, Edgar, the Fool, Albany, and, most important, an anonymous servant) define nature as a network and hierarchy of relationships having definite obligations and responsibilities. Furthermore, these "natural" relationships are based on love and respect, not fear and oppression. They define and "place" the individual even while they recognize and affirm the fellowship and commonality of mankind. They are lawful relationships because they maintain social harmony and nurture life. Smash these bonds, the play tells us, and the result is exile, madness, inhuman torture, and death.

King Lear is a gloomy play, so unremittingly ironic and sorrowful, in fact, that the unsentimental Dr. Samuel Johnson could not bear to re-read its conclusion. Seeing Lear carrying the dead Cordelia, Kent asks with incredulous dismay, "Is this the promised end?" His question is our own. Is this the end of the world, the end and purpose of life? Is this dreadful sight a symbolic total of all our hopeful acts? We would like to think not. Yet at the play's end we have witnessed a slaughter. Cornwall, Goneril, Regan, Edmund, Cordelia, are killed by violence; Gloucester's "flawed heart" has burst; and Lear is dead from grief, too long stretched "upon the rack of this tough world." The Fool has disappeared, and Kent, as he himself predicts, will soon join Lear in death. What justice is here? What can we say for mankind if this is the "promised end"?

There is hope, but not much. And it is this small hope that is the central experience of the play. At the conclusion of *King Lear* the evil characters, those who violated or misunderstood the bonds of nature and society, are dead. Those who maintained those bonds did so at the cost of suffering and even death. Only Edgar, Albany, and Kent (temporarily) escape with their lives. The chaos of war and murderous destruction initiated by an unwitting Lear have subsided and been replaced by the sober and almost cryptic demand for candor expressed by Edgar: "The weight of this sad time we must obey; / Speak what we feel, not what we ought to say."

Thus the play concludes in somber tragedy with the crushing weight of a "sad time." But for all of its compelling sorrow, the end also sounds a minor though insistent note of heartening victory and promise. We can say with some confidence that the play *contains within it* the seeds of hope. Let us consider these questions: What force or influence brings about the downfall of Edmund and his party? Why, when they seem to have all the *power*, when their opponents are weak, degraded, in exile, when Lear is mad, the King's retinue scattered, Edgar and Kent in lowly disguise—why are Edmund and the rest overcome?

They are *not* defeated by divine intervention, despite the efforts of some critics to prove the contrary. *King Lear* is relentlessly secular, a tragedy of mortals acting from human motives. The defeated fall by the very principles they have used to justify their acts, by the egocentricity Lear first displays and which is shared by Goneril, Regan, Edmund, and Cornwall. None of these characters believes in a lawful or "natural" community of mankind. (The King later changes his attitudes, but only after intense suffering.) None believe in those harmonious relationships that generate compassion, loyalty, and honesty. Regarding all others as enemies, they act from motives of fear and hatred, and by means of force. As they serve others, so are they served. Thus Goneril and Regan deceive and are fatally deceived. Cornwall's arrogant viciousness exceeds the bounds of humanity and leads to his own death. The evidence of that viciousness helps to destroy the others. Edmund, so certain of the primacy of power, so sure of the weaknesses of legitimacy, is ironically unmasked and killed while arrogantly toying with the very forms of lawfulness he so despises. The evil characters feed on themselves. Living without love for others, only for power *over* others, they are made vulnerable and eventually destroyed by their own principles.

Given this interpretation of *King Lear*—that evil results from a violation of the fundamental relationships binding us together, and that people who violate those bonds not only destroy others but are also destroyed by their own acts—how might it be applied to a dramatization?

If the interpretation is valid, it will assist the reader in imagining every one of a play's thousand visual and auditory details. It will, moreover, allow the reader to function as a director, to "orchestrate," as it were, the play's momentum and plot, emphasizing certain scenes and speeches as especially illustrative of the primary interpretation.

Three specific scenes both illuminate and enforce our interpretation, and thus should be stressed, not only because they are among the most dramatic scenes in *King Lear* and all of Shakespeare, but because the information they contain should be placed firmly and emphatically in our minds, whether we are reading or seeing the play. Two of these scenes take place in the middle of the action, in Act Three, and both concern the two fathers, Lear and Gloucester, at low psychological points: Lear insane on the stormy heath (Act Three, Scene IV), and Gloucester blinded by Cornwall (Act Three, Scene VII). The third significant scene, the Trial by Combat between the illegitimate Edmund and the legitimate Edgar, occurs at the end of the play (Act Five, Scene III).

The scene on the heath is fairly simple in outline. Lear, Kent, and the Fool are on stage, commenting on the fierceness of the storm and the ingratitude of Goneril and Regan. Edgar disguised as the mad Tom o' Bedlam enters, and Lear compares himself and all men to the nearly naked Tom. Then Gloucester enters, tells the group that he will lead them to food and shelter, and mentions that he, too, suffers from the filial ingratitude of the now outlawed Edgar. The scene ends with all the characters going off to find shelter.

This bare narrative does not begin to describe the richness of the scene and its relation to the play's central experience. Right away we learn from Kent that the storm and "the tyranny of the open night's too rough for *nature* to endure" (emphasis added). In other words, being out of doors on such a night is unnatural; yet Lear has been driven there by his daughters. The King says he is oblivious to the weather, for he has a tempest in his mind. The unnaturalness of his daughters afflicts him more than the storm. He describes and questions their cruelty with a metaphor that succinctly and powerfully underscores their violation of the physical bonds between parent and child. "Filial ingratitude! Is it not as this mouth should tear this hand for lifting food to 't?"

A few lines later, while encouraging the Fool to take shelter in a nearby hovel, Lear recognizes his kinship and kingly obligation to all men, and his neglect of that bond and responsibility:

> Poor naked wretches, wheresoe'er you are,
> That bide the pelting of this pitiless storm,
> How shall your houseless heads and unfed sides,
> Your loop'd and window'd raggedness, defend you
> From seasons such as these? O! I have ta'en
> Too little care of this. Take physic, pomp;
> Expose thyself to feel what wretches feel,
> That thou mayst shake the superflux to them,
> And show the heavens more just.

This compassionate self-awareness is broken by the appearance of Tom o' Bedlam, whose seeming madness reminds Lear of the tempestuous thoughts caused by the cruel unkindness of his daughters. Finally, after listening to Tom's wise yet raving talk and looking on Tom's wretched nakedness, Lear perceives the essential frailty of all men when stripped of their borrowings. As he says to the madman, "Thou art the thing itself; unaccommodated man is no more but such a poor, bare, forked animal as thou art." Then, wishing to reach that most basic level of man, the "thing itself," Lear begins to strip himself of his borrowings, the clothes he owes to the creatures in nature that provide him with raiment: "Off, off, you lendings! Come; unbutton here."

At this point Gloucester enters, seeking the King to lead him to "where both fire and food is ready." This elemental act of kindness is not performed without courage. Goneril and Regan now seek Lear's death, and by thwarting them Gloucester runs a great risk. But he takes the chance, finds the courage, because he feels compassion for the old man and an obligation toward him as his king. "Go in with me," he begs Lear. "My duty cannot suffer / To obey in all your daughters' hard commands." By disobeying the "hard commands" and "injunctions" of those who wield power, and by following the compassionate promptings of his duty, Gloucester saves the King's life.

Because it is so natural, so human, and because most of us think we, too, would shelter the suffering Lear, Gloucester's selflessness goes almost unnoticed by us in the audience. But it has significant consequences. After learning from the treacherous Edmund that Gloucester is in communication with the forces of France and that he has assisted Lear, Cornwall and Regan blind Gloucester in one of the most violent and terrifying scenes in all of dramatic literature.

The scene, although painful and almost unbearable (some directors stage the eye-gouging out of sight of the audience), is more than merely sensational. It clarifies the desperate fury of Cornwall and Regan, draws a line beyond which inhuman and unnatural behavior cannot go unchallenged, and creates a great pivot point upon which the whole action of the play turns.

The ferocity of the daughters and Cornwall opens the scene. Anticipating the apprehension of Gloucester, Regan says, "Hang him instantly." Goneril, suggesting a mutilation that remains in the mind of Cornwall (and perhaps in the minds of the audience), would "Pluck out his eyes." Cornwall, at first uncertain of the punishment he would inflict upon Gloucester, is nevertheless determined on some obscene cruelty. He sends Edmund away because "the revenges we are bound to take upon your traitorous father are not fit for your beholding." To add to the terror of the moment, this determined savagery is compounded with calculated lawlessness. Cornwall knows he cannot kill Gloucester "Without the form of justice," but he will bend his power to the demands of his overriding anger in such a way as to inflict a hurt but evade the constraints of law. "Our power," he states, "shall do a courts'y to our wrath, which men / May blame, but not control." Though he may not murder Gloucester, he can do worse, and injure him.

The injury is excruciating to witness, for loss of sight is a universal fear that all of us share as Cornwall rips an eye from the tormented yet resolute Gloucester. As Cornwall reaches for the second eye, we wish to cry out, "Stop!" The inhumanity of the act, its vicious excess, the pain and loss touch us at our deepest levels. Just then an anonymous character, designated only as "First Servant," is moved to act. We exclaim with him:

> Hold your hand, my lord.
> I have served you ever since I was a child,
> But better service have I never done you
> Than now to bid you hold.

Up to this point in the play, the malevolent and grasping have swept all before them, but here a line is drawn. The blinding of Gloucester is of such elemental inhumanity that the First Servant *cannot* allow it to continue, *no matter what* the cost. And his spontaneous intercession puts him in great danger. He is a mere servant, an anonymous nobody, low in the social hierarchy, seemingly powerless. Yet he chooses to challenge a powerful and angry master whom he has served since childhood. This single act of mercy and courage of an unknown "Everyman" turns the play in a new direction.

At first, the Servant's bravery seems to have been fruitless. He is fatally stabbed from behind by Regan; Cornwall, although mortally wounded, snatches out Gloucester's second eye. But the effect of the event, however small, is evident immediately. The other servants resolve to assist those oppressed by the malefactors and agree to help the bleeding Gloucester. One goes to find Tom o' Bedlam as a guide for the blind man; the other to fetch "some flax and whites of egg / To apply to his bleeding face." Thus this horrific scene ends on a note of humane and homely generosity, of specific, active compassion.

The effects of Gloucester's blinding continue after the event. We find Albany, unresolved but already disaffected by the news of Lear's flight and madness, speculating on the meaning and end of the unnatural, "barbarous," and "degenerate" actions of Goneril, Regan, and Cornwall:

> If that the heavens do not their visible spirits
> Send quickly down to tame these vile offenses,
> It will come,
> Humanity must perforce prey on itself,
> Like monsters of the deep.

While musing on this pessimistic thought and in a state of troubled inaction, he learns of Cornwall's death and of the First Servant's brave but mortal challenge. Albany regards this news as evidence of divine justice: "This shows you are above, / You justicers, that these our nether crimes / So speedily can venge!" Upon asking if Gloucester lost his other eye, he is answered by the Messenger: "Both, both, my lord." Then learning that Edmund betrayed his blind father, "and quit the house on purpose, that their punishment might have the freer course," Albany resolves *himself* to be a justicer: "Gloucester, I live / To thank thee for the love thou show'dst the king, / And to revenge thine eyes."

What we recognize in Albany's final resolution is that the "visible spirits" he had hoped for come not from heaven but from earth. The First Servant, acting from *human,* not divine, impulse, fatally but successfully resisted Cornwall's "vile offenses" against humankind. The Servant's example, together with the news of Edmund's "offenses," persuades Albany to act, to tame the vicious and unjust, to halt the spectacle of humanity, preying on itself "like monsters of the deep," and to wait no longer for a divine intercession that may not come.

Like the First Servant and Albany, others, when learning of Gloucester's mutilation, respond with pity for the Earl and defiance of the malefactors. Regan knows this when she tells the Steward Oswald, "It was great ignorance, Gloucester's eyes being out, to let him live; where he arrives he moves all hearts against us." The blind man is tangible evidence of the cruel ways of the oppressors. He should be killed, put out of sight and mind. Regan, in fact, tells Oswald, "If you do chance to hear of that blind traitor, / Preferment falls on him that cuts him off." Happening upon Gloucester and his guide the disguised Edgar, Oswald confidently prepares to kill the Earl whose "eyeless head" he believes "was first framed flesh to raise my fortunes." But Edgar interposes, kills Oswald, and finds a letter from Goneril to Edmund that will ironically be the means of bringing the unkind and unnatural to bloody justice.

Thus the blinding of Gloucester, as searing as it is for the audience, has a clear thematic purpose. Their inhuman act, performed with the arrogant assurance of power, is precisely the cause that eventually destroys Cornwall, Regan, and their confederates. Moreover, Edmund's contempt for the order of society, for its customs and laws, results in his destruction, too.

Having won the battle against the French forces, having captured and arranged for the deaths of Cordelia and Lear, and being adulterously and illicitly desired by both Goneril and Regan, Edmund seems at the top of his powers. What can stop his unscrupulous career now? He has risen from bastardy to an earldom, and, as seems likely if he marries either of the daughters, he will soon control half a kingdom. Just at this supreme moment of triumph he is arrested and challenged.

The challenge is not casual or formless, but framed in the ceremonious language of the law. When Albany arrests Edmund "On capital treason," the charge is delivered openly and in full, as if a legal officer were speaking in a court of justice. After the charge, a form of trial ensues, a trial by combat. Albany and Edmund exchange pledges, a trumpet sounds, a Herald reads the formal charge and challenge, the trumpet sounds twice more, and the disguised Edgar as challenger appears. He is interrogated as to name and rank, refuses to give his name, but asserts he is as "noble as the adversary I come to cope." Continuing the formal ritual of the trial, Edgar confronts his adversary directly and accuses Edmund of treason, "a traitor, / False to thy gods, thy brother, and thy father," and a conspirator against Albany.

Edmund's answer is characteristically contemptuous of custom and rule. Because his challenger is anonymous, Edmund might correctly ask his name and thereby avoid or delay the combat. (A knight was not obliged to fight beneath his rank.) Instead he answers: "What safe and nicely I might well delay / By rule of knighthood I disdain and spurn." He denies the charges, fights with Edgar, and falls mortally wounded.

Thus the Trial by Combat (a legal though neglected judicial procedure in Shakespeare's time) results in a just verdict. Edgar's sword, arm, and best spirits prove Edmund's guilt, a fact that

Edmund duly confesses: "What you have charged me with, that I have done, / And more, much more; the time will bring it out." The lawless Edmund is therefore checked by the law, by the ritual forms and customary procedures he held in such contempt. The irony of his death, equal to that of Cornwall's, Goneril's, and Regan's, reminds us of the biblical injunction: "They that take the sword shall perish with the sword."

All this is not to say that we can rest complacently in the thought that the evil of the world will perforce eat itself up. There are costs to pay, and resistance to malevolent power is frail and tenuous. Cordelia dies before Edmund can send word countermanding his order for her death and Lear's. The King survives her briefly, then dies of sorrow. Gloucester is dead, Kent disconsolate, and the kingdom momentarily without leadership. The conclusion is funereal. "Our present business," says Albany, "is general woe."

Despite this oppressive weight of sorrow, we remember the actions of those who maintained their humanity and courage in a time of dark and dangerous terror: Kent's dauntless loyalty, Edgar's filial compassion, Gloucester's duty and fortitude, Cordelia's gentle and redeeming love, and above all, the anonymous First Servant's thrilling courage. He stands as an example for us all. Having no power, no rank, he is nevertheless a man, and therefore recognizes without the benefit of law books the blinding of Gloucester as an inhuman crime against another man. He does not stop to consider the consequences of his protest, does not think to stand by uninvolved. He simply acts, motivated by the demands of his own humanity. He ignores the danger to himself when he says to his violent master, "Hold your hand, my lord." How many of us would do the same? We might hesitate and think such a gesture either foolhardy or inconsequential. But in this play we see how a single act of moral courage has effects of startling magnitude. We all are capable of being "justicers," if only we have the courage.

It would be beyond the intention of this essay to show how each scene and character in the play should conform to our central thesis, but it is possible to remark on some of the major figures. Lear is an old but strong man. Age (but not senility) and arrogance are conditions of his personality, but so is his understandable yet disastrous need for an articulate expression of his daughters' love. Such a desire is natural to all parents. And most parents, I suspect, would feel Lear's disappointment with Cordelia's statement, but most would not and could not, of course, express that disappointment with such sudden and crushing power. The wish might be there, but the monarchical habit and weight of command would not.

Gloucester, the other father, should appear as a benevolent but, like Lear, occasionally thoughtless man. His credulity results from his essential good nature, his willingness to trust and be trusted. His is a fearful and untried virtue, but when it comes to the test, he is equal to the demands and, more important, capable of learning the lessons of adversity. After his blinding, he says to his disguised son, "I stumbled when I saw. Full oft 'tis seen, / Our means secure us, and our mere defects / Prove our commodities."

Edmund is a difficult character. He is both attractive and repellent. We admire his intellect and resourcefulness but deplore the deceitful principles to which they are devoted. We can sympathize with the fundamental injustice of his bastardy, but we cannot condone the inhumane and hypocritical means he employs to escape and avenge his condition. But overall, Edmund should repel us. He is moral ugliness masked by intellectual brilliance. Because he cares only for himself, he cannot be trusted and therefore cannot be loved.

The other characters, Kent, Edgar, Cordelia, Albany, Oswald, Goneril, Regan, Cornwall, although rich in personal nuance, are, with the possible exception of Edgar, less ambiguous than Edmund or the two fathers. They tend to fall logically onto one side or the other of an opposition of good and evil.

The way characters are assembled has an important effect on the force or emphasis of a scene. Merely a few examples can be cited here, although the drawings that accompany the following text will suggest pertinent and possible dramatic groupings. Only at the beginning and end of the play are all the characters together, and the action in both instances is ceremonious—the dividing of the kingdom, and the trial by combat. The scenes in between are peopled by fragments of the whole, thus mirroring the action of a drama that starts in ceremonious order, plunges into the formless chaos of madness, exile, torture, conspiracy, and war, then concludes with order precariously restored, but only at a terrible price, as demonstrated by the scarcity of the survivors. The beginning and ending scenes should therefore be formal and balanced, assembled in similar patterns to remind us of the seeming order at the beginning and the disastrously recovered order of the conclusion.

Because our interpretation of the play emphasizes the blinding of Gloucester, this terrible event should not be softened. The bloody details should be painfully evident, for the intention is not merely to horrify but to create a desire in the viewer to cry out with the First Servant, "Hold your hand, my lord."

In Shakespeare's plays, certain gestures grow, as it were, out of the lines themselves; and they are generally meant to emphasize a detail in the actor's speech that contributes to the immediate meaning of the action. Because characters cannot move on a page to draw attention to themselves or their words, we have supplied visual details where an actor might use a gesture for emphasis. Lear in his various forms, from regal dominance to humble "foolish fond old man," is depicted. So, too, are Edgar disguised as the mad Tom o' Bedlam, Gloucester's bleeding eye-sockets, Regan's violent hand driving a sword through the First Servant, Cordelia's forgiving posture as she attends her revived father.

The tone of particular speeches and scenes is perhaps impossible to convey by visual means alone. The human voice creates tone. Inflection, pitch, stress, cadence—these and other characteristics of speech communicate subtle degrees and mixtures of anger, remorse, determination—in short, all of the emotions we can feel, and all of the emotions a skilled playwright can rouse in us. Yet a drawing of a face in sorrow or a fist clenched in anger can at least suggest the general tone in which a particular speech is heard. These and other visual devices are used throughout the text to create tonality and mood both in specific scenes and for the play as a whole.

A great play performed by great actors is an unforgettable event. For a brief time we enter another world, one that is both familiar and strange. It is familiar because it contains human beings who move and speak as we do. It is strange because the human problems the characters confront are condensed yet heightened, and therefore intensified, by the powerful illusions of art. We see on the stage our own experience, our own longings and disappointments, but experience stripped of the confusion of local and personal details. We perceive the fundamental elements of our humanity. We learn what it means to be human.

It is to this end that the following text is dedicated, for nothing is more important than to find out what we are.

KING LEAR

Dramatis Personae

LEAR, *King of Britain.*

KING OF FRANCE.

DUKE OF BURGUNDY.

DUKE OF CORNWALL, *Husband to Regan.*

DUKE OF ALBANY, *Husband to Goneril.*

EARL OF KENT.

EARL OF GLOUCESTER.

EDGAR, *Son to Gloucester.*

EDMUND, *Bastard Son to Gloucester.*

CURAN, *a Courtier.*

OSWALD, *Steward to Goneril.*

Old Man, Tenant to Gloucester.

Doctor.

Fool.

An Officer, employed by Edmund.

Gentleman, Attendant on Cordelia.

A Herald.

Servants to Cornwall.

GONERIL,
REGAN,   } *Daughters to Lear.*
CORDELIA,

Knights of Lear's train, Officers, Messengers, Soldiers, and Attendants.

SCENE: *Britain.*

knave came something saucily into the world before he was sent for, yet was his mother fair; there was good sport at his making, and the whoreson must be acknowledged. Do you know this noble gentleman, Edmund?

EDMUND.   No, my lord.

GLOUCESTER.   My Lord of Kent: remember him hereafter as my honorable friend.

EDMUND.   My services to your lordship.

KENT.   I must love you, and sue to know you better.

EDMUND.   Sir, I shall study deserving.

GLOUCESTER.   He hath been out nine years, and away he shall again. The king is coming.

Sennet. Enter one bearing a coronet, KING LEAR, CORNWALL, ALBANY, GONERIL, REGAN, CORDELIA, *and Attendants.*

LEAR.   Attend the lords of France and Burgundy, Gloucester.

GLOUCESTER.   I shall, my liege.

Exeunt GLOUCESTER *and* EDMUND.

LEAR.   Meantime, we shall express our darker purpose.
             Give me the map there. Know that we have divided
             In three our kingdom; and 'tis our fast intent
             To shake all cares and business from our age,
             Conferring them on younger strengths, while we
             Unburden'd crawl toward death. Our son of Cornwall,
             And you, our no less loving son of Albany,
             We have this hour a constant will to publish
             Our daughters' several dowers, that future strife

ACT ONE

SCENE I.   *A State Room in King Lear's Palace.*

Enter KENT, GLOUCESTER, *and* EDMUND.

KENT. I thought the king had more affected the Duke of
Albany than Cornwall.

GLOUCESTER. It did always seem so to us; but now, in the
division of the kingdom, it appears not which of the dukes he values
most; for equalities are so weighed that curiosity in neither can make
choice of either's moiety.

KENT. Is not this your son, my lord?

GLOUCESTER. His breeding, sir, hath been at my charge: I have
so often blushed to acknowledge him, that now I am brazed to it.

KENT. I cannot conceive you.

GLOUCESTER. Sir, this young fellow's mother could; whereupon
she grew round-wombed, and had, indeed, sir, a son for her cradle
ere she had a husband for her bed. Do you smell a fault?

KENT. I cannot wish the fault undone, the issue of it being so
proper.

GLOUCESTER. But I have a son, sir, by order of law, some year
older than this, who yet is no dearer in my account: though this

3

May be prevented now. The princes, France and Bur-
 gundy,
Great rivals in our youngest daughter's love,
Long in our court have made their amorous sojourn,
And here are to be answer'd. Tell me, my daughters,
Since now we will divest us both of rule,
Interest of territory, cares of state,
Which of you shall we say doth love us most?
That we our largest bounty may extend
Where nature doth with merit challenge. Goneril,
Our eldest-born, speak first.

GONERIL. Sir, I do love you more than words can wield the matter;
Dearer than eyesight, space and liberty;
Beyond what can be valued rich or rare;
No less than life, with grace, health, beauty, honor;
As much as child e'er lov'd, or father found;
A love that makes breath poor and speech unable;
Beyond all manner of so much I love you.

CORDELIA [aside]. What shall Cordelia do? Love, and be silent.

LEAR. Of all these bounds, even from this line to this, with
shadowy forests and with champains rich'd, with plenteous rivers
and wide-skirted meads, we make thee lady: to thine and Albany's
issue be this perpetual. What says our second daughter, our dearest
Regan, wife to Cornwall? Speak.

REGAN.　I am made of that self metal as my sister,
　　　　　And prize me at her worth. In my true heart
　　　　　I find she names my very deed of love;
　　　　　Only she comes too short: that I profess
　　　　　Myself an enemy to all other joys
　　　　　Which the most precious square of sense possesses,
　　　　　And find I am alone felicitate
　　　　　In your dear highness' love.

CORDELIA [aside].　Then poor Cordelia! And yet not so; since I am sure my love's more ponderous than my tongue.

LEAR.　To thee and thine, hereditary ever, remain this ample third of our fair kingdom, no less in space, validity, and pleasure, than that conferr'd on Goneril. Now, our joy, although the last, not least; to whose young love the vines of France and milk of Burgundy strive to be interess'd; what can you say to draw a third more opulent than your sisters? Speak.

CORDELIA.　Nothing, my lord.

LEAR.　Nothing?

CORDELIA.　Nothing.

LEAR.　Nothing will come of nothing: speak again.

CORDELIA.　Unhappy that I am, I cannot heave my heart into my mouth: I love your majesty according to my bond; no more nor less.

LEAR.　How, how, Cordelia! mend your speech a little, lest you may mar your fortunes.

CORDELIA.　Good my lord,
　　　　　You have begot me, bred me, lov'd me: I
　　　　　Return those duties back as are right fit,　　·
　　　　　Obey you, love you, and most honor you.
　　　　　Why have my sisters husbands, if they say
　　　　　They love you all? Haply, when I shall wed,
　　　　　That lord whose hand must take my plight shall carry
　　　　　Half my love with him, half my care and duty:
　　　　　Sure I shall never marry like my sisters,
　　　　　To love my father all.

LEAR.　But goes thy heart with this?

CORDELIA.　Ay, my good lord.

LEAR.　So young, and so untender?

CORDELIA.　So young, my lord, and true.

LEAR. Let it be so; thy truth then be thy dower:
For, by the sacred radiance of the sun,
The mysteries of Hecate and the night,
By all the operation of the orbs
From whom we do exist and cease to be,
Here I disclaim all my paternal care,
Propinquity and property of blood,
And as a stranger to my heart and me
Hold thee from this for ever. The barbarous Scythian,
Or he that makes his generation messes
To gorge his appetite, shall to my bosom
Be as well neighbor'd, pitied, and relieved,
As thou my sometime daughter.

KENT. Good my liege—

LEAR. Peace, Kent! Come not between the dragon and his
wrath. I loved her most, and thought to set my rest on her kind
nursery. Hence, and avoid my sight! So be my grave my peace, as
here I give her father's heart from her! Call France. Who stirs? Call

Burgundy. Cornwall and Albany, with my two daughters' dowers digest this third; let pride, which she calls plainness, marry her. I do invest you jointly in my power, pre-eminence, and all the large effects that troop with majesty. Ourself, by monthly course, with reservation of an hundred knights by you to be sustain'd, shall our abode make with you by due turn. Only we still retain the name and all the additions to a king; the sway, revenue, execution of the rest, beloved sons, be yours: which to confirm, this coronet part betwixt you.

    KENT.   Royal Lear, whom I have ever honor'd as my king, loved as my father, as my master follow'd, as my great patron thought on in my prayers—

    LEAR.   The bow is bent and drawn; make from the shaft.

    KENT.   Let it fall rather, though the fork invade the region of my heart: be Kent unmannerly, when Lear is mad. What would'st thou do, old man? Think'st thou that duty shall have dread to speak

when power to flattery bows? To plainness honor's bound when
majesty falls to folly. Reserve thy state; and, in thy best consideration, check this hideous rashness: answer my life my judgment, thy
youngest daughter does not love thee least; nor are those empty-
hearted whose low sound reverbs no hollowness.

LEAR.   Kent, on thy life, no more.

KENT.   My life I never held but as a pawn to wage against thine
enemies; nor fear to lose it, thy safety being the motive.

LEAR.   Out of my sight!

KENT.   See better, Lear; and let me still remain the true blank
of thine eye.

LEAR.   Now, by Apollo—

KENT.   Now, by Apollo, king, thou swear'st thy gods in vain.

LEAR. O, vassal! miscreant! *Laying his hand upon his sword.*

ALBANY, CORNWALL. Dear sir, forbear.

KENT. Do; kill thy physician, and the fee bestow upon the foul disease. Revoke thy doom; or, whilst I can vent clamor from my throat, I'll tell thee thou dost evil.

LEAR.   Hear me, recreant!
            On thine allegiance, hear me!
            Since thou hast sought to make us break our vow,
            Which we durst never yet, and with strain'd pride
            To come betwixt our sentence and our power,
            Which nor our nature nor our place can bear,
            Our potency made good, take thy reward.
            Five days we do allot thee for provision
            To shield thee from diseases of the world;
            And on the sixth to turn thy hated back
            Upon our kingdom: if on the tenth day following

Thy banish'd trunk be found in our dominions,
The moment is thy death. Away! By Jupiter,
This shall not be revok'd.

KENT.   Fare thee well, king; sith thus thou wilt appear, freedom
lives hence, and banishment is here. [*To* CORDELIA] The gods to their
dear shelter take thee, maid, that justly think'st and hast most rightly
said! [*To* GONERIL *and* REGAN] And your large speeches may your
deeds approve, that good effects may spring from words of love. Thus
Kent, O princes! bids you all adieu; he'll shape his old course in a
country new.   *Exit.*

Flourish. Re-enter GLOUCESTER, *with* FRANCE, BURGUNDY, *and*
Attendants.

GLOUCESTER.   Here's France and Burgundy, my noble lord.

LEAR.   My Lord of Burgundy, we first address toward you, who
with this king hath rivall'd for our daughter. What, in the least, will
you require in present dower with her, or cease your quest of love?

BURGUNDY.   Most royal majesty, I crave no more than what
your highness offer'd, nor will you tender less.

LEAR.   Right noble Burgundy, when she was dear to us we did
hold her so, but now her price is fall'n. Sir, there she stands: if aught
within that little-seeming substance, or all of it, with our displeasure
pieced, and nothing more, may fitly like your grace, she's there, and
she is yours.

BURGUNDY.   I know no answer.

LEAR. Will you, with those infirmities she owes, unfriended,
new-adopted to our hate, dower'd with our curse and stranger'd with
our oath, take her, or leave her?

BURGUNDY. Pardon me, royal sir; election makes not up on
such conditions.

LEAR. Then leave her, sir; for, by the power that made me, I
tell you all her wealth. [*To* FRANCE] For you, great king, I would not
from your love make such a stray to match you where I hate;
therefore beseech you to avert your liking a more worthier way than

on a wretch whom nature is ashamed almost to acknowledge hers.

FRANCE. This is most strange, that she, that even but now was
your best object, the argument of your praise, balm of your age, most
best, most dearest, should in this trice of time commit a thing so
monstrous, to dismantle so many folds of favor. Sure, her offense
must be of such unnatural degree that monsters it, or your
fore-vouch'd affection fall'n into taint; which to believe of ner, must
be a faith that reason without miracle should never plant in me.

CORDELIA. I yet beseech your majesty, (if for I want that glib
and oily art to speak and purpose not, since what I well intend, I'll
do 't before I speak), that you make known it is no vicious blot,
murder or foulness, no unchaste action, or dishonor'd step, that hath
deprived me of your grace and favor, but even for want of that for
which I am richer, a still-soliciting eye, and such a tongue that I am
glad I have not, though not to have it hath lost me in your liking.

LEAR. Better thou hadst not been born than not to have pleased me better.

FRANCE. Is it but this? a tardiness in nature which often leaves the history unspoke that it intends to do? My Lord of Burgundy, what say you to the lady? Love's not love when it is mingled with regards that stand aloof from the entire point. Will you have her? she is herself a dowry.

BURGUNDY. Royal Lear, give but that portion which yourself proposed, and here I take Cordelia by the hand, duchess of Burgundy.

LEAR. Nothing: I have sworn; I am firm.

BURGUNDY. I am sorry, then, you have so lost a father that you must lose a husband.

CORDELIA. Peace be with Burgundy! Since that respects of fortune are his love, I shall not be his wife.

FRANCE. Fairest Cordelia, that art most rich, being poor; most choice, forsaken; and most loved, despised! Thee and thy virtues here I seize upon: be it lawful I take up what's cast away. Gods, gods! 'tis strange that from their cold'st neglect my love should kindle to inflamed respect. Thy dowerless daughter, king, thrown to my chance, is queen of us, of ours, and our fair France: not all the dukes of waterish Burgundy shall buy this unprized precious maid of

me. Bid them farewell, Cordelia, though unkind: thou losest here, a
better where to find.

LEAR.   Thou hast her, France; let her be thine, for we have no
such daughter, nor shall ever see that face of hers again; therefore be
gone without our grace, our love, our benison. Come, noble
Burgundy.

Flourish.   Exeunt LEAR,   BURGUNDY,   CORNWALL,   ALBANY,
GLOUCESTER, *and Attendants.*

FRANCE. Bid farewell to your sisters.

CORDELIA. The jewels of our father, with wash'd eyes Cordelia leaves you: I know you what you are; and like a sister am most loth to call your faults as they are named. Use well our father: to your professed bosoms I commit him: but yet, alas! stood I within his grace, I would prefer him to a better place. So farewell to you both.

REGAN. Prescribe not us our duties.

GONERIL. Let your study be to content your lord, who hath receiv'd you at fortune's alms; you have obedience scanted, and well are worth the want that you have wanted.

CORDELIA. Time shall unfold what plighted cunning hides; who cover faults, at last shame them derides. Well may you prosper!

FRANCE. Come, my fair Cordelia.

Exeunt FRANCE *and* CORDELIA.

GONERIL. Sister, it is not little I have to say of what most nearly appertains to us both. I think our father will hence tonight.

REGAN. That's most certain, and with you; next month with us.

GONERIL. You see how full of changes his age is; the observation we have made of it hath not been little: he always loved our sister most; and with what poor judgment he hath now cast her off appears too grossly.

REGAN. 'Tis the infirmity of his age; yet he hath ever but slenderly known himself.

GONERIL. The best and soundest of his time hath been but rash; then must we look to receive from his age, not alone the imperfections of long-engraffed condition, but therewithal the unruly waywardness that infirm and choleric years bring with them.

REGAN. Such unconstant starts are we like to have from him as this of Kent's banishment.

GONERIL. There is further compliment of leave-taking between France and him. Pray you, let's hit together: if our father carry authority with such disposition as he bears, this last surrender of his will but offend us.

REGAN. We shall further think on 't.

GONERIL. We must do something, and i' th' heat. *Exeunt.*

SCENE II.   *A Hall in the Earl of Gloucester's Castle.*

Enter EDMUND, *with a letter.*

EDMUND.   Thou, Nature, art my goddess; to thy law
My services are bound. Wherefore should I
Stand in the plague of custom, and permit
The curiosity of nations to deprive me,
For that I am some twelve or fourteen moonshines
Lag of a brother? Why bastard? wherefore base?
When my dimensions are as well compact,
My mind as generous, and my shape as true,
As honest madam's issue? Why brand they us
With base? with baseness? bastardy? base, base?
Who in the lusty stealth of nature take
More composition and fierce quality
Than doth, within a dull, stale, tired bed,
Go to the creating a whole tribe of fops,
Got 'tween asleep and wake? Well then,
Legitimate Edgar, I must have your land:
Our father's love is to the bastard Edmund
As to the legitimate. Fine word, "legitimate"!
Well, my legitimate, if this letter speed,
And my invention thrive, Edmund the base
Shall top the legitimate—: I grow, I prosper;
Now, gods, stand up for bastards!

17

Enter GLOUCESTER.

GLOUCESTER.   Kent banish'd thus! And France in choler parted!
And the king gone tonight! subscribed his power! Confin'd to
exhibition! All this done upon the gad!—Edmund, how now! what
news?

EDMUND.   So please your lordship, none. *Putting up the letter.*

GLOUCESTER.   Why so earnestly seek you to put up that letter?

EDMUND.   I know no news, my lord.

GLOUCESTER.   What paper were you reading?

EDMUND.   Nothing, my lord.

GLOUCESTER.   No? What needed then that terrible dispatch of
it into your pocket? the quality of nothing hath not much need to
hide itself. Let's see: come; if it be nothing, I shall not need
spectacles.

EDMUND.   I beseech you, sir, pardon me; it is a letter from my
brother that I have not all o'erread, and for so much as I have
perused, I find it not fit for your o'erlooking.

GLOUCESTER.   Give me the letter, sir.

EDMUND.   I shall offend, either to detain or give it. The
contents, as in part I understand them, are to blame.

GLOUCESTER.   Let's see, let's see.

EDMUND.   I hope, for my brother's justification, he wrote this
but as an essay or taste of my virtue.

GLOUCESTER [*reads*].   "This policy and reverence of age makes
the world bitter to the best of our times; keeps our fortunes from us
till our oldness cannot relish them. I begin to find an idle and fond
bondage in the oppression of aged tyranny, who sways, not as it hath
power, but as it is suffered. Come to me, that of this I may speak

more. If our father would sleep till I wake him, you should enjoy half his revenue for ever, and live the beloved of your brother,   Edgar."

Hum! Conspiracy! "Sleep till I wake him—you should enjoy half his revenue." My son Edgar! Had he a hand to write this? a heart and brain to breed it in? When came this to you? Who brought it?

EDMUND.   It was not brought me, my lord; there's the cunning of it; I found it thrown in at the casement of my closet.

GLOUCESTER.   You know the character to be your brother's?

EDMUND.   If the matter were good, my lord, I durst swear it were his; but, in respect of that, I would fain think it were not.

GLOUCESTER.   It is his.

EDMUND.   It is his hand, my lord; but I hope his heart is not in the contents.

GLOUCESTER.   Has he never before sounded you in this business?

EDMUND.   Never, my lord: but I have heard him oft maintain it

to be fit that, sons at perfect age, and fathers declined, the father
should be as ward to the son, and the son manage his revenue.

GLOUCESTER.   O villain, villain! His very opinion in the letter!
Abhorred villain! Unnatural, detested, brutish villain! worse than
brutish! Go, sirrah, seek him; ay apprehend him. Abominable villain!
Where is he?

EDMUND.   I do not well know, my lord. If it shall please you to
suspend your indignation against my brother till you can derive from
him better testimony of his intent, you shall run a certain course;
where, if you violently proceed against him, mistaking his purpose, it
would make a great gap in your own honor, and shake in pieces the
heart of his obedience. I dare pawn down my life for him, that he
hath wrote this to feel my affection to your honor, and to no other
pretense of danger.

GLOUCESTER.   Think you so?

EDMUND.   If your honor judge it meet, I will place you where
you shall hear us confer of this, and by an auricular assurance have
your satisfaction; and that without any further delay than this very
evening.

GLOUCESTER.   He cannot be such a monster—

EDMUND.   Nor is not, sure.

GLOUCESTER.   —to his father, that so tenderly and entirely loves
him. Heaven and earth! Edmund, seek him out; wind me into him, I
pray you: frame the business after your own wisdom. I would unstate
myself to be in a due resolution.

EDMUND.   I will seek him, sir, presently; convey the business as
I shall find means, and acquaint you withal.

GLOUCESTER.   These late eclipses in the sun and moon portend
no good to us: though the wisdom of nature can reason it thus and
thus, yet nature finds itself scourged by the sequent effects. Love
cools, friendship falls off, brothers divide: in cities, mutinies; in
countries, discord; in palaces, treason; and the bond cracked 'twixt
son and father. This villain of mine comes under the prediction;
there's son against father: the king falls from bias of nature; there's
father against child. We have seen the best of our time: machina-
tions, hollowness, treachery, and all ruinous disorders follow us
disquietly to our graves. Find out this villain, Edmund; it shall lose
thee nothing: do it carefully. And the noble and true-hearted Kent
banished! his offense, honesty! 'Tis strange.   *Exit.*

EDMUND.   This is the excellent foppery of the world, that, when we are sick in fortune, often the surfeit of our own behavior, we make guilty of our disasters the sun, the moon, and the stars; as if we were villains on necessity, fools by heavenly compulsion, knaves, thieves, and treachers by spherical predominance, drunkards, liars, and adulterers by an enforced obedience of planetary influence; and all that we are evil in, by a divine thrusting on. An admirable evasion of whoremaster man, to lay his goatish disposition to the charge of a star! My father compounded with my mother under the dragon's tail, and my nativity was under Ursa major; so that it follows I am rough and lecherous. Fut! I should have been that I am had the maidenliest star in the firmament twinkled on my bastardizing. Edgar— [*Enter* EDGAR] and pat he comes, like the catastrophe of the old comedy: my

cue is villainous melancholy, with a sigh like Tom o' Bedlam. O!
these eclipses do portend these divisions. Fa, sol, la, mi.

EDGAR.   How now, brother Edmund! What serious contemplation are you in?

EDMUND.   I am thinking, brother, of a prediction I read this
other day, what should follow these eclipses.

EDGAR.   Do you busy yourself with that?

EDMUND.   I promise you the effects he writes of succeed
unhappily; as of unnaturalness between the child and the parent;
death, dearth, dissolutions of ancient amities; divisions in state;
menaces and maledictions against king and nobles; needless diffiden-
ces, banishment of friends, dissipation of cohorts, nuptial breaches,
and I know not what.

EDGAR.   How long have you been a sectary astronomical?

EDMUND.   Come, come; when saw you my father last?

EDGAR.   The night gone by.

EDMUND.   Spake you with him?

EDGAR.   Ay, two hours together.

EDMUND.   Parted you in good terms? Found you no displeasure
in him by word nor countenance?

EDGAR.   None at all.

EDMUND.   Bethink yourself wherein you may have offended
him; and at my entreaty forbear his presence until some little time
hath qualified the heat of his displeasure, which at this instant so
rageth in him that with the mischief of your person it would scarcely
allay.

EDGAR.   Some villain hath done me wrong.

EDMUND.   That's my fear, brother. I pray you have a continent
forbearance till the speed of his rage goes slower, and as I say, retire
with me to my lodging, from whence I will fitly bring you to hear my
lord speak. Pray you, go; there's my key. If you do stir abroad, go
armed.

EDGAR.   Armed, brother!

EDMUND.   Brother, I advise you to the best, go armed; I am no
honest man if there be any good meaning towards you; I have told
you what I have seen and heard; but faintly, nothing like the image
and horror of it; pray you, away.

EDGAR.   Shall I hear from you anon?

EDMUND.   I do serve you in this business. [*Exit* EDGAR.] A

credulous father, and a brother noble, whose nature is so far from doing harms that he suspects none; on whose foolish honesty my practices ride easy! I see the business. Let me, if not by birth, have lands by wit: all with me 's meet that I can fashion fit.   *Exit.*

SCENE III.

A Room in the Duke of Albany's Palace.

Enter GONERIL, *and* OSWALD, *her Steward.*

GONERIL.   Did my father strike my gentleman for chiding of his fool?

OSWALD.   Ay, madam.

GONERIL.   By day and night he wrongs me; every hour he flashes into one gross crime or other, that sets us all at odds: I'll not endure it: his knights grow riotous, and himself upbraids us on every trifle. When he returns from hunting I will not speak with him; say I am sick: if you come slack of former services, you shall do well; the fault of it I'll answer.

OSWALD.   He's coming, madam; I hear him.   *Horns within.*

GONERIL.   Put on what weary negligence you please, you and your fellows; I'd have it come to question: if he distaste it, let him to our sister, whose mind and mine, I know, in that are one, not to be overrul'd. Idle old man, that still would manage those authorities that he hath given away! Now, by my life, old fools are babes again, and must be used with checks as flatteries, when they are seen abused. Remember what I have said.

OSWALD.   Very well, madam.

GONERIL.   And let his knights have colder looks among you; what grows of it, no matter; advise your fellows so: I would breed from hence occasions, and I shall, that I may speak: I'll write straight to my sister to hold my very course. Prepare for dinner.   *Exeunt.*

SCENE IV.   *A Hall in the Same.*

Enter KENT, *disguised.*

KENT. If but as well I other accents borrow, that can my speech defuse, my good intent may carry through itself to that full issue for which I razed my likeness. Now, banish'd Kent, if thou canst serve where thou dost stand condemn'd, so may it come, thy master, whom thou lovest, shall find thee full of labors.

Horns within. Enter LEAR, *Knights, and Attendants.*

LEAR. Let me not stay a jot for dinner: go, get it ready. *[Exit an Attendant.]* How now! what art thou?

KENT. A man, sir.

LEAR. What dost thou profess? What would'st thou with us?

KENT. I do profess to be no less than I seem; to serve him truly that will put me in trust; to love him that is honest; to converse with him that is wise, and says little; to fear judgment; to fight when I cannot choose; and to eat no fish.

LEAR. What art thou?

KENT. A very honest-hearted fellow, and as poor as the king.

25

LEAR.   If thou be as poor for a subject as he is for a king, thou
art poor enough. What would'st thou?

KENT.   Service.

LEAR.   Who would'st thou serve?

KENT.   You.

LEAR.   Dost thou know me, fellow?

KENT.   No, sir; but you have that in your countenance which I
would fain call master.

LEAR.   What's that?

KENT.   Authority.

LEAR.   What services canst thou do?

KENT.   I can keep honest counsel, ride, run, mar a curious tale
in telling it, and deliver a plain message bluntly; that which ordinary
men are fit for, I am qualified in, and the best of me is diligence.

LEAR.   How old art thou?

KENT.   Not so young, sir, to love a woman for singing, nor so old
to dote on her for anything; I have years on my back forty-eight.

LEAR.   Follow me; thou shalt serve me: if I like thee no worse
after dinner I will not part from thee yet. Dinner, ho! dinner!
Where's my knave? my fool? Go you and call my fool hither.

Exit an Attendant.

Enter OSWALD.

You, you, sirrah, where's my daughter?

OSWALD.   So please you—   *Exit.*

LEAR.   What says the fellow there? Call the clotpoll back. *[Exit
a Knight.]* Where's my fool, ho? I think the world's asleep. *[Re-enter
Knight.]* How now! where's that mongrel?

KNIGHT.   He says, my lord, your daughter is not well.

LEAR.   Why came not the slave back to me when I called him?

KNIGHT.   Sir, he answered me in the roundest manner, he
would not.

LEAR.   He would not!

KNIGHT.   My lord, I know not what the matter is; but, to my
judgment, your highness is not entertained with that ceremonious
affection as you were wont; there's a great abatement of kindness
appears as well in the general dependants as in the duke himself also
and your daughter.

LEAR.   Ha! sayest thou so?

KNIGHT.   I beseech you, pardon me, my lord, if I be mistaken; for my duty cannot be silent when I think your highness wronged.

LEAR.   Thou but rememberest me of mine own conception: I have perceived a most faint neglect of late; which I have rather blamed as mine own jealous curiosity than as a very pretense and purpose of unkindness: I will look further into 't. But where's my fool? I have not seen him this two days.

KNIGHT.   Since my young lady's going into France, sir, the fool hath much pined away.

LEAR.   No more of that; I have noted it well. Go you, and tell my daughter I would speak with her. *[Exit an Attendant.]* Go you, call hither my fool.   *Exit an Attendant.*

Re-enter OSWALD.

O! you sir, you sir, come you hither, sir. Who am I, sir?

OSWALD.   My lady's father.

LEAR.   "My lady's father"! my lord's knave: you whoreson dog! you slave! you cur!

OSWALD.   I am none of these, my lord; I beseech your pardon.

LEAR.   Do you bandy looks with me, you rascal? *Striking him.*

OSWALD.   I'll not be strucken, my lord.

KENT.   Nor tripped neither, you base football player. *Tripping up his heels.*

LEAR.   I thank thee, fellow; thou servest me, and I'll love thee.

KENT.   Come, sir, arise, away! I'll teach you differences: away, away! If you will measure your lubber's length again, tarry; but away! Go to; have you wisdom? so.   *Pushes* OSWALD *out.*

LEAR.   Now, my friendly knave, I thank thee: there's earnest of thy service.   *Gives* KENT *money.*

Enter Fool.

FOOL. Let me hire him too: here's my coxcomb.

Offers KENT *his cap.*

LEAR. How now, my pretty knave! how dost thou?

FOOL. Sirrah, you were best take my coxcomb.

KENT. Why, fool?

FOOL. Why? for taking one's part that's out of favor. Nay, an thou canst not smile as the wind sits, thou'lt catch cold shortly: there, take my coxcomb. Why, this fellow has banished two on's daughters, and did the third a blessing against his will: if thou follow him thou must needs wear my coxcomb. How now, nuncle! Would I had two coxcombs and two daughters!

LEAR. Why, my boy?

FOOL. If I gave them all my living, I'd keep my coxcombs myself. There's mine; beg another of thy daughters.

LEAR. Take heed, sirrah; the whip.

FOOL. Truth's a dog must to kennel; he must be whipped out when Lady the brach may stand by the fire and stink.

LEAR. A pestilent gall to me!

FOOL. Sirrah, I'll teach thee a speech.

LEAR. Do.

FOOL. Mark it, nuncle:

> *Have more than thou showest,*
> *Speak less than thou knowest,*
> *Lend less than thou owest,*
> *Ride more than thou goest,*
> *Learn more than thou trowest,*
> *Set less than thou throwest;*
> *Leave thy drink and thy whore,*
> *And keep in-a-door,*
> *And thou shalt have more*
> *Than two tens to a score.*

KENT. This is nothing, fool.

FOOL. Then 'tis like the breath of an unfee'd lawyer; you gave me nothing for 't. Can you make no use of nothing, nuncle?

LEAR. Why, no, boy; nothing can be made out of nothing.

FOOL [*to* KENT]. Prithee, tell him, so much the rent of his land comes to: he will not believe a fool.

LEAR. A bitter fool!

FOOL.   Dost thou know the difference, my boy, between a bitter fool and a sweet fool?

LEAR.   No, lad; teach me.

FOOL.
>   *That lord that counsell'd thee*
>   *To give away thy land,*
>   *Come place him here by me,*
>   *Do thou for him stand:*
>   *The sweet and bitter fool*
>   *Will presently appear;*
>   *The one in motley here,*
>   *The other found out there.*

LEAR.   Dost thou call me fool, boy?

FOOL.   All thy other titles thou hast given away; that thou wast born with.

KENT.   This is not altogether fool, my lord.

FOOL.   No, faith, lords and great men will not let me; if I had a monopoly out, they would have part on 't: and ladies too, they will not let me have all the fool to myself; they'll be snatching. Nuncle, give me an egg, and I'll give thee two crowns.

LEAR.   What two crowns shall they be?

FOOL.   Why, after I have cut the egg i' the middle and eat up the meat, the two crowns of the egg. When thou clovest thy crown i' the middle, and gavest away both parts, thou borest thine ass on thy back o'er the dirt: thou hadst little wit in thy bald crown when thou gavest thy golden one away. If I speak like myself in this, let him be whipped that first finds it so.

>   *Fools had ne'er less grace in a year;*
>   *For wise men are grown foppish,*
>   *And know not how their wits to wear,*
>   *Their manners are so apish.*

LEAR.   When were you wont to be so full of songs, sirrah?

FOOL.   I have used it, nuncle, ever since thou madest thy daughters thy mothers; for when thou gavest them the rod and puttest down thine own breeches,

>   *Then they for sudden joy did weep,*
>   *And I for sorrow sung,*
>   *That such a king should play bo-peep,*
>   *And go the fools among.*

Prithee, nuncle, keep a schoolmaster that can teach thy fool to lie: I would fain learn to lie.

LEAR.   An you lie, sirrah, we'll have you whipped.

FOOL.   I marvel what kin thou and thy daughters are: they'll have me whipped for speaking true, thou 'lt have me whipped for lying; and sometimes I am whipped for holding my peace. I had rather be any kind o' thing than a fool; and yet I would not be thee, nuncle; thou hast pared thy wit o' both sides, and left nothing i' the middle: here comes one o' the parings.

Enter GONERIL.

LEAR.   How now, daughter! what makes that frontlet on? Methinks you are too much of late i' the frown.

FOOL.   Thou wast a pretty fellow when thou hadst no need to care for her frowning; now thou art an O without a figure. I am

better than thou art now; I am a fool, thou art nothing. [*To* GONERIL] Yes, forsooth, I will hold my tongue; so your face bids me, though you say nothing.

> *Mum, mum:*
> *He that keeps nor crust nor crum,*
> *Weary of all, shall want some.*

That's a shealed peascod.   *Pointing to* LEAR.

GONERIL. Not only, sir, this your all-licens'd fool, but other of your insolent retinue do hourly carp and quarrel, breaking forth in rank and not-to-be-endured riots. Sir, I had thought, by making this well known unto you, to have found a safe redress; but now grow fearful, by what yourself too late have spoke and done, that you protect this course, and put it on by your allowance; which if you should, the fault would not 'scape censure, nor the redresses sleep, which, in the tender of a wholesome weal, might in their working do you that offense, which else were shame, that then necessity will call discreet proceeding.

FOOL. For you know, nuncle,

> *The hedge-sparrow fed the cuckoo so long,*
> *That it had it head bit off by it young.*

So out went the candle, and we were left darkling.

LEAR. Are you our daughter?

GONERIL. Come, sir, I would you would make use of that good

wisdom, whereof I know you are fraught; and put away these
dispositions which of late transport you from what you rightly are.

FOOL. May not an ass know when a cart draws the horse?
Whoop, Jug! I love thee.

LEAR. Doth any here know me? This is not Lear: does Lear
walk thus? speak thus? Where are his eyes? Either his notion
weakens, or 's discernings are lethargied. Ha! waking? 'tis not so.
Who is it that can tell me who I am?

FOOL. Lear's shadow.

LEAR. I would learn that; for by the marks of sovereignty,
knowledge, and reason, I should be false persuaded I had daughters.

FOOL. Which they will make an obedient father.

LEAR. Your name, fair gentlewoman?

GONERIL. This admiration, sir, is much o' the savor of other
your new pranks. I do beseech you to understand my purposes
aright: as you are old and reverend, should be wise. Here do you
keep a hundred knights and squires; men so disorder'd, so debosh'd,
and bold, that this our court, infected with their manners, shows like
a riotous inn: epicurism and lust makes it more like a tavern or a
brothel than a graced palace. The shame itself doth speak for instant
remedy; be then desired by her, that else will take the thing she begs,
a little to disquantity your train; and the remainder, that shall still
depend, to be such men as may besort your age, which know
themselves and you.

LEAR. Darkness and devils! Saddle my horses; call my train
together. Degenerate bastard! I'll not trouble thee: yet have I left a
daughter.

GONERIL. You strike my people, and your disorder'd rabble
make servants of their betters.

                                                        Enter ALBANY.

LEAR.   Woe, that too late repents; O! sir, are you come?
               Is it your will? Speak, sir. Prepare my horses.
               Ingratitude, thou marble-hearted fiend,
               More hideous, when thou show'st thee in a child,
               Than the sea-monster.

ALBANY. Pray, sir, be patient.

LEAR [*to* GONERIL].

               Detested kite! thou liest:
               My train are men of choice and rarest parts,

That all particulars of duty know,
And in the most exact regard support
The worships of their name. O most small fault,
How ugly didst thou in Cordelia show!
Which, like an engine, wrench'd my frame of nature
From the fix'd place, drew from my heart all love,
And added to the gall. O Lear, Lear, Lear!
Beat at this gate, that let thy folly in, *[Striking his head.]*
And thy dear judgment out! Go, go, my people.

ALBANY.   My lord, I am guiltless, as I am ignorant of what hath
moved you.

LEAR.   It may be so, my lord.
              Hear, Nature, hear! dear goddess, hear!
              Suspend thy purpose, if thou didst intend
              To make this creature fruitful!
              Into her womb convey sterility!
              Dry up in her the organs of increase,

And from her derogate body never spring
A babe to honor her! If she must teem,
Create her child of spleen, that it may live
And be a thwart disnatured torment to her!
Let it stamp wrinkles in her brow of youth,
With cadent tears fret channels in her cheeks,
Turn all her mother's pains and benefits
To laughter and contempt, that she may feel
How sharper than a serpent's tooth it is
To have a thankless child! Away, away!   *Exit.*

ALBANY.   Now, gods that we adore, whereof comes this?

GONERIL.   Never afflict yourself to know the cause; but let his disposition have that scope that dotage gives it.

Re-enter LEAR.

LEAR.   What! fifty of my followers at a clap; within a fortnight!

ALBANY.   What's the matter, sir?

LEAR.   I'll tell thee. [*To* GONERIL] Life and death! I am asham'd that thou hast power to shake my manhood thus, that these hot tears, which break from me perforce, should make thee worth them. Blasts and fogs upon thee! The untented woundings of a father's curse pierce every sense about thee! Old fond eyes, beweep this cause again, I'll pluck ye out, and cast you, with the waters that you lose, to

temper clay. Yea, is it come to this? Let it be so: I have another daughter, who, I am sure, is kind and comfortable: when she shall hear this of thee, with her nails she'll flay thy wolvish visage. Thou shalt find that I'll resume the shape which thou dost think I have cast off for ever; thou shalt, I warrant thee.

Exeunt LEAR, KENT, *and Attendants.*

GONERIL.   Do you mark that, my lord?

ALBANY.   I cannot be so partial, Goneril, to the great love I bear you—

GONERIL.   Pray you, content. What, Oswald, ho! *[To the Fool]* You, sir, more knave than fool, after your master.

FOOL.   Nuncle Lear, nuncle Lear! tarry, and take the fool with thee.

> *A fox, when one has caught her,*
>   *And such a daughter,*
> *Should sure to the slaughter,*
>   *If my cap would buy a halter;*
> *So the fool follows after.*   *Exit.*

GONERIL.   This man hath had good counsel. A hundred knights! 'Tis politic and safe to let him keep at point a hundred knights; yes,

that on every dream, each buzz, each fancy, each complaint, dislike, he may enguard his dotage with their powers, and hold our lives in mercy. Oswald, I say!

ALBANY.   Well, you may fear too far.

GONERIL.   Safer than trust too far. Let me still take away the harms I fear, not fear still to be taken: I know his heart. What he hath utter'd I have writ my sister; if she sustain him and his hundred knights, when I have show'd the unfitness—[*Re-enter* OSWALD] How now, Oswald! What, have you writ that letter to my sister?

OSWALD.   Ay, madam.

GONERIL.   Take you some company, and away to horse: inform her full of my particular fear; and thereto add such reasons of your own as may compact it more. Get you gone, and hasten your return. [*Exit* OSWALD.] No, no, my lord, this milky gentleness and course of yours though I condemn it not, yet, under pardon, you are much more attask'd for want of wisdom than praised for harmful mildness.

ALBANY.   How far your eyes may pierce I cannot tell: striving to better, oft we mar what's well.

GONERIL.   Nay, then—

ALBANY.   Well, well; the event.   *Exeunt.*

SCENE V.   *Court before the Same.*

Enter LEAR, KENT, *and Fool.*

LEAR. Go you before to Gloucester with these letters. Acquaint my daughter no further with anything you know than comes from her demand out of the letter. If your diligence be not speedy I shall be there afore you.

KENT. I will not sleep, my lord, till I have delivered your letter.

Exit.

FOOL. If a man's brain were in 's heels, were 't not in danger of kibes?

LEAR. Ay, boy.

FOOL. Then, I prithee, be merry; thy wit shall ne'er go slip-shod.

LEAR. Ha, ha, ha!

FOOL. Shalt see thy other daughter will use thee kindly; for though she's as like this as a crab's like an apple, yet I can tell what I can tell.

LEAR. What canst tell, boy?

FOOL. She will taste as like this as a crab does to a crab. Thou canst tell why one's nose stands i' the middle on 's face?

LEAR. No.

FOOL. Why, to keep one's eyes of either side's nose, that what a man cannot smell out, he may spy into.

LEAR. I did her wrong—

FOOL. Canst tell how an oyster makes his shell?

LEAR. No.

FOOL. Nor I neither; but I can tell why a snail has a house.

LEAR.   Why?

FOOL.   Why, to put 's head in; not to give it away to his daughters, and leave his horns without a case.

LEAR.   I will forget my nature. So kind a father! Be my horses ready?

FOOL.   Thy asses are gone about 'em. The reason why the seven stars are no more than seven is a pretty reason.

LEAR.   Because they are not eight?

FOOL.   Yes, indeed: thou would'st make a good fool.

LEAR.   To take 't again perforce! Monster ingratitude!

FOOL.   If thou wert my fool, nuncle, I'd have thee beaten for being old before thy time.

LEAR.   How's that?

FOOL.   Thou should'st not have been old till thou hadst been wise.

LEAR.   O! let me not be mad, not mad, sweet heaven; keep me in temper; I would not be mad! *[Enter Gentleman]* How now! Are the horses ready?

GENTLEMAN.   Ready, my lord.

LEAR.   Come, boy.

FOOL.   She that's a maid now, and laughs at my departure, shall not be a maid long, unless things be cut shorter.   *Exeunt.*

ACT TWO

SCENE I.   *A Court within the Castle of the Earl of Gloucester.*

Enter EDMUND *and* CURAN, *meeting.*

EDMUND.   Save thee, Curan.

CURAN.   And you, sir. I have been with your father, and given him notice that the Duke of Cornwall and Regan his duchess will be here with him this night.

EDMUND.   How comes that?

CURAN.   Nay, I know not. You have heard of the news abroad? I mean the whispered ones, for they are yet but ear-kissing arguments.

EDMUND.   Not I: pray you, what are they?

CURAN.   Have you heard of no likely wars toward, 'twixt the Dukes of Cornwall and Albany?

EDMUND.   Not a word.

CURAN.   You may do then, in time. Fare you well, sir.   *Exit.*

EDMUND.   The duke be here to-night! The better! best! This weaves itself perforce into my business. My father hath set guard to take my brother; and I have one thing, of a queasy question, which I must act. Briefness and fortune, work! Brother, a word; descend: brother, I say! [*Enter* EDGAR] My father watches: O sir! fly this place; intelligence is given where you are hid; you have now the good advantage of the night. Have you not spoken 'gainst the Duke of Cornwall? He's coming hither, now, i' the night, i' the haste, and Regan with him; have you nothing said upon his party 'gainst the Duke of Albany? Advise yourself.

42

EDGAR.   I am sure on 't, not a word.

EDMUND.   I hear my father coming; pardon me; in cunning I must draw my sword upon you; draw; seem to defend yourself; now quit you well. Yield; come before my father. Light, ho! here! Fly, brother. Torches! torches! So, farewell. [*Exit* EDGAR.] Some blood drawn on me would beget opinion [*Wounds his arm*] of my more fierce endeavor: I have seen drunkards do more than this in sport. Father! father! Stop, stop! No help?

Enter GLOUCESTER, *and Servants with torches.*

GLOUCESTER.   Now, Edmund, where's the villain?

EDMUND.   Here stood he in the dark, his sharp sword out,

mumbling of wicked charms, conjuring the moon to stand's auspicious mistress.

GLOUCESTER.   But where is he?

EDMUND.   Look, sir, I bleed.

GLOUCESTER.   Where is the villain, Edmund?

EDMUND.   Fled this way, sir. When by no means he could—

GLOUCESTER.   Pursue him, ho! Go after. *[Exeunt some Servants.]* "By no means" what?

EDMUND.   Persuade me to the murder of your lordship;
But that I told him, the revenging gods
'Gainst parricides did all their thunders bend;
Spoke with how manifold and strong a bond
The child was bound to the father; sir, in fine,
Seeing how loathly opposite I stood
To his unnatural purpose, in fell motion,
With his prepared sword he charges home
My unprovided body, lanced mine arm:
But when he saw my best alarum'd spirits
Bold in the quarrel's right, roused to the encounter,
Or whether gasted by the noise I made,
Full suddenly he fled.

GLOUCESTER.   Let him fly far: not in this land shall he remain uncaught; and found—dispatch. The noble duke my master, my worthy arch and patron, comes tonight: by his authority I will proclaim it, that he which finds him shall deserve our thanks, bringing the murderous coward to the stake; he that conceals him, death.

EDMUND.   When I dissuaded him from his intent, and found him pight to do it, with curst speech I threaten'd to discover him: he replied, "Thou unpossessing bastard! dost thou think, if I would stand against thee, would the reposal of any trust, virtue, or worth in thee make thy words faith'd? No: what I should deny—as this I would; ay, though thou didst produce my very character, I'd turn it all to thy suggestion, plot, and damned practice: and thou must make a dullard of the world, if they not thought the profits of my death were very pregnant and potential spurs to make thee seek it."

GLOUCESTER.   Strange and fasten'd villain! Would he deny his letter? I never got him. *[Tucket within.]* Hark! the duke's trumpets. I know not why he comes. All ports I'll bar; the villain shall not 'scape;

the duke must grant me that: besides his picture I will send far and near, that all the kingdom may have due note of him; and of my land, loyal and natural boy, I'll work the means to make thee capable.

Enter CORNWALL, REGAN, *and Attendants.*

CORNWALL.   How now, my noble friend! since I came hither, which I can call but now, I have heard strange news.

REGAN.   If it be true, all vengeance comes too short which can pursue the offender. How dost, my lord?

GLOUCESTER.   O! madam, my old heart is crack'd, is crack'd.

REGAN.   What! did my father's godson seek your life? He whom my father named, your Edgar?

GLOUCESTER.   O! lady, lady, shame would have it hid.

REGAN.   Was he not companion with the riotous knights that tend upon my father?

GLOUCESTER.   I know not, madam; 'tis too bad, too bad.

EDMUND.   Yes, madam, he was of that consort.

REGAN. No marvel then though he were ill affected; 'tis they have put him on the old man's death, to have the expense and waste of his revenues. I have this present evening from my sister been well inform'd of them, and with such cautions that if they come to sojourn at my house, I'll not be there.

CORNWALL. Nor I, assure thee, Regan. Edmund, I hear that you have shown your father a childlike office.

EDMUND. 'Twas my duty, sir.

GLOUCESTER. He did bewray his practice; and received this hurt you see, striving to apprehend him.

CORNWALL. Is he pursued?

GLOUCESTER. Ay, my good lord.

CORNWALL. If he be taken he shall never more be fear'd of doing harm; make your own purpose, how in my strength you please. For you, Edmund, whose virtue and obedience doth this instant so much commend itself, you shall be ours: natures of such deep trust we shall much need; you we first seize on.

EDMUND. I shall serve you, sir, truly, however else.

GLOUCESTER. For him I thank your grace.

CORNWALL. You know not why we came to visit you—

REGAN. Thus out of season, threading dark-eyed night: occasions, noble Gloucester, of some poise. Wherein we must have use of your advice. Our father he hath writ, so hath our sister, of differences, which I best thought it fit to answer from our home; the several messengers from hence attend dispatch. Our good old friend, lay comforts to your bosom, and bestow your needful counsel to our business, which craves the instant use.

GLOUCESTER. I serve you, madam. Your graces are right welcome. *Flourish. Exeunt.*

SCENE II.   *Before Gloucester's Castle.*

Enter KENT *and* OSWALD, *severally.*

OSWALD. Good dawning to thee, friend: art of this house?

KENT. Ay.

OSWALD. Where may we set our horses?

KENT. I' the mire.

OSWALD. Prithee, if thou lovest me, tell me.

KENT. I love thee not.

OSWALD. Why, then I care not for thee.

KENT. If I had thee in Lipsbury pinfold, I would make thee care for me.

OSWALD. Why dost thou use me thus? I know thee not.

KENT. Fellow, I know thee.

OSWALD. What dost thou know me for?

KENT. A knave, a rascal, an eater of broken meats; a base, proud, shallow, beggarly, three-suited, hundred-pound, filthy worsted-stocking knave; a lily-livered, action-taking knave; a whoreson, glass-gazing, super-serviceable, finical rogue; one-trunk-inheriting slave; one that wouldst be a bawd in way of good service, and art nothing but the composition of a knave, beggar, coward, pander, and the son and heir of a mongrel bitch: one whom I will beat into clamorous whining if thou deniest the least syllable of thy addition.

OSWALD. Why, what a monstrous fellow art thou, thus to rail on one that is neither known of thee nor knows thee!

KENT. What a brazen-faced varlet art thou, to deny thou knowest me! Is it two days since I tripped up thy heels and beat thee

48

before the king? Draw, you rogue; for though it be night, yet the moon shines: I'll make a sop o' the moonshine of you. *[Drawing his sword.]* Draw, you whoreson cullionly barber-monger, draw.

OSWALD.   Away! I have nothing to do with thee.

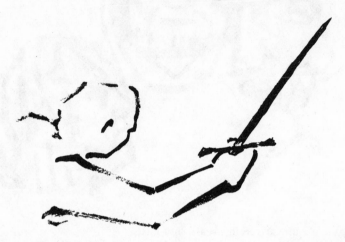

KENT.   Draw, you rascal; you come with letters against the king, and take Vanity the puppet's part against the royalty of her father. Draw, you rogue, or I'll so carbonado your shanks: draw, you rascal; come your ways.

OSWALD.   Help, ho! murder! help!

KENT.   Strike, you slave; stand, rogue, stand; you neat slave, strike.   *Beats him.*

OSWALD.   Help, ho! murder! murder!

Enter EDMUND, with his rapier drawn.

EDMUND.   How now! What's the matter?   *Parts them.*

KENT.   With you, goodman boy, an you please: come, I'll flesh ye; come on, young master.

Enter CORNWALL, REGAN, GLOUCESTER, and Servants.

GLOUCESTER.   Weapons! arms! What's the matter here?

CORNWALL.   Keep peace, upon your lives: he dies that strikes again. What is the matter?

REGAN.   The messengers from our sister and the king.

CORNWALL.   What is your difference? speak.

OSWALD. I am scarce in breath, my lord.

KENT. No marvel, you have so bestirred your valor. You cowardly rascal, nature disclaims in thee: a tailor made thee.

CORNWALL. Thou art a strange fellow; a tailor make a man?

KENT. Ay, a tailor, sir: a stonecutter or a painter could not have made him so ill, though they had been but two hours at the trade.

CORNWALL. Speak yet, how grew your quarrel?

OSWALD. This ancient ruffian, sir, whose life I have spared at suit of his gray beard—

KENT. Thou whoreson zed! thou unnecessary letter! My lord, if you will give me leave, I will tread this unbolted villain into mortar, and daub the wall of a jakes with him. Spare my gray beard, you wagtail?

CORNWALL. Peace, sirrah! You beastly knave, know you no reverence?

KENT. Yes, sir; but anger hath a privilege.

CORNWALL. Why art thou angry?

KENT.   That such a slave as this should wear a sword,
            Who wears no honesty. Such smiling rogues as these,
            Like rats, oft bite the holy cords a-twain

Which are too intrinse t' unloose; smooth every passion
That in the natures of their lords rebel;
Bring oil to fire, snow to their colder moods;
Renege, affirm, and turn their halcyon beaks
With every gale and vary of their masters,
Knowing nought, like dogs, but following.
A plague upon your epileptic visage!
Smile you my speeches, as I were a fool?
Goose, if I had you upon Sarum plain,
I'd drive ye cackling home to Camelot.

CORNWALL.   What! art thou mad, old fellow?

GLOUCESTER.   How fell you out? say that.

KENT.   No contraries hold more antipathy than I and such a knave.

CORNWALL.   Why dost thou call him knave? What is his fault?

KENT.   His countenance likes me not.

CORNWALL.   No more, perchance, does mine, nor his, nor hers.

KENT.   Sir, 'tis my occupation to be plain: I have seen better faces in my time than stands on any shoulder that I see before me at this instant.

CORNWALL.   This is some fellow, who, having been praised for bluntness, doth affect a saucy roughness, and constrains the garb quite from his nature: he cannot flatter, he, an honest mind and plain, he must speak truth: an they will take it, so; if not, he's plain. These kind of knaves I know, which in this plainness harbor more craft and more corrupter ends than twenty silly-ducking observants, that stretch their duties nicely.

KENT.   Sir, in good faith, in sincere verity, under the allowance of your great aspect, whose influence, like the wreath of radiant fire on flickering Phœbus' front—

CORNWALL.   What mean'st by this?

KENT.   To go out of my dialect, which you discommend so much. I know, sir, I am no flatterer: he that beguiled you in a plain accent was a plain knave; which for my part I will not be, though I should win your displeasure to entreat me to 't.

CORNWALL.   What was the offense you gave him?

OSWALD.   I never gave him any: it pleased the king his master very late to strike at me, upon his misconstruction; when he, conjunct, and flattering his displeasure, tripp'd me behind; being down, insulted, rail'd, and put upon him such a deal of man, that worthied him, got praises of the king for him attempting who was self-subdu'd; and, in the fleshment of this dread exploit, drew on me here again.

KENT.   None of these rogues and cowards but Ajax is their fool.

CORNWALL.   Fetch forth the stocks! You stubborn-ancient knave, you reverend braggart, we'll teach you.

KENT.   Sir, I am too old to learn. Call not your stocks for me; I serve the king, on whose employment I was sent to you; you shall do small respect, show too bold malice against the grace and person of my master, stocking his messenger.

CORNWALL.   Fetch forth the stocks! As I have life and honor, there shall he sit till noon.

REGAN.   Till noon! till night, my lord; and all night too.

KENT.   Why, madam, if I were your father's dog, you should not use me so.

REGAN.   Sir, being his knave, I will.

CORNWALL.   This is a fellow of the self-same color our sister speaks of. Come, bring away the stocks.   *Stocks brought out.*

GLOUCESTER.   Let me beseech your grace not to do so. His fault

is much, and the good king his master will check him for 't: your
purposed low correction is such as basest and contemned'st wretches
for pilferings and most common trespasses are punish'd with: the
king must take it ill, that he, so slightly valued in his messenger,
should have him thus restrain'd.

CORNWALL. I'll answer that.

REGAN. My sister may receive it much more worse to have her
gentleman abused, assaulted, for following her affairs. Put in his legs.
[KENT *is put in the stocks.*] Come, my good lord, away.

Exeunt all but GLOUCESTER *and* KENT.

GLOUCESTER. I am sorry for thee, friend; 'tis the duke's
pleasure, whose disposition, all the world well knows, will not be
rubb'd nor stopp'd: I'll entreat for thee.

KENT. Pray, do not, sir. I have watch'd and travell'd hard;
some time I shall sleep out, the rest I'll whistle. A good man's fortune
may grow out at heels: give you good morrow!

GLOUCESTER. The duke's to blame in this; 'twill be ill taken.

Exit.

KENT. Good king, that must approve the common saw, thou
out of heaven's benediction comest to the warm sun! Approach, thou
beacon to this under globe, that by thy comfortable beams I may
peruse this letter. Nothing almost sees miracles, but misery: I know
'tis from Cordelia, who hath most fortunately been inform'd of my
obscured course; and shall find time from this enormous state,
seeking to give losses their remedies. All weary and o'erwatch'd, take
vantage, heavy eyes, not to behold this shameful lodging. Fortune,
good night; smile once more; turn thy wheel!   *He sleeps.*

SCENE III.   *A Wood.*

Enter EDGAR.

EDGAR.   I heard myself proclaim'd; and by the happy hollow of a tree escaped the hunt. No port is free; no place, that guard, and most unusual vigilance, does not attend my taking. Whiles I may 'scape, I will preserve myself; and am bethought to take the basest and most poorest shape that ever penury, in contempt of man, brought near to beast; my face I'll grime with filth, blanket my loins, elf all my hair in knots, and with presented nakedness outface the winds and persecutions of the sky. The country gives me proof and precedent of Bedlam beggars, who, with roaring voices, strike in their numb'd and mortified bare arms pins, wooden pricks, nails, sprigs of rosemary; and with this horrible object, from low farms, poor pelting villages, sheepcotes, and mills, sometime with lunatic bans, sometime with prayers, enforce their charity. Poor Turlygod! poor Tom! That's something yet: Edgar I nothing am.   *Exit.*

SCENE IV.   *Before Gloucester's Castle. Kent in the Stocks.*

Enter LEAR, *Fool, and Gentleman.*

LEAR.   'Tis strange that they should so depart from home, and not send back my messenger.

GENTLEMAN.   As I learn'd, the night before there was no purpose in them of this remove.

KENT.   Hail to thee, noble master!

LEAR.   Ha! Makest thou this shame thy pastime?

KENT.   No, my lord.

FOOL.   Ha, ha! he wears cruel garters. Horses are tied by the heads, dogs and bears by the neck, monkeys by the loins, and men by the legs: when a man's over-lusty at legs, then he wears wooden nether-stocks.

LEAR.   What's he that hath so much thy place mistook to set thee here?

KENT.   It is both he and she, your son and daughter.

LEAR.   No.

KENT.   Yes.

LEAR.   No, I say.

KENT.   I say, yea.

LEAR.   No, no; they would not.

KENT.   Yes, they have.

LEAR.   By Jupiter, I swear, no.

KENT.   By Juno, I swear, ay.

LEAR.   They durst not do 't; they could not, would not do 't; 'tis

55

worse than murder, to do upon respect such violent outrage. Resolve me, with all modest haste, which way thou might'st deserve, or they impose, this usage, coming from us.

KENT. My lord, when at their home I did commend your highness' letters to them, ere I was risen from the place that show'd my duty kneeling, came there a reeking post, stew'd in his haste, half breathless, panting forth from Goneril his mistress salutations; deliver'd letters, spite of intermission, which presently they read: on whose contents they summon'd up their meiny, straight took horse; commanded me to follow, and attend the leisure of their answer; gave me cold looks: and meeting here the other messenger, whose welcome, I perceived, had poison'd mine, being the very fellow which of late display'd so saucily against your highness, having more man than wit about me, drew: he raised the house with loud and coward cries. Your son and daughter found this trespass worth the shame which here it suffers.

FOOL. Winter's not gone yet, if the wild geese fly that way.

> *Fathers that wear rags*
> *Do make their children blind,*
> *But fathers that bear bags*
> *Shall see their children kind.*
> *Fortune, that arrant whore,*
> *Ne'er turns the key to the poor.*

But for all this thou shalt have as many dolors for thy daughters as thou canst tell in a year.

LEAR. O! how this mother swells up toward my heart. *Hysterica passio!* down, thou climbing sorrow! Thy element's below. Where is this daughter?

KENT. With the earl, sir; here within.

LEAR. Follow me not; stay here.   *Exit.*

GENTLEMAN. Made you no more offense but what you speak of?

KENT. None. How chance the king comes with so small a number?

FOOL. An thou hadst been set i' the stocks for that question, thou hadst well deserved it.

KENT. Why, fool?

FOOL. We'll set thee to school to an ant, to teach thee there's no laboring i' the winter. All that follow their noses are led by their eyes but blind men; and there's not a nose among twenty but can smell him that's stinking. Let go thy hold when a great wheel runs down a hill, lest it break thy neck with following it; but the great one that goes up the hill, let him draw thee after. When a wise man gives thee better counsel, give me mine again: I would have none but knaves follow it, since a fool gives it.

> *That sir which serves and seeks for gain,*
>   *And follows but for form,*
> *Will pack when it begins to rain,*
>   *And leave thee in the storm.*
> *But I will tarry; the fool will stay,*
>   *And let the wise man fly:*
> *The knave turns fool that runs away;*
>   *The fool no knave, perdy.*

KENT.   Where learned you this, fool?

FOOL.   Not i' the stocks, fool.

Re-enter LEAR, *with* GLOUCESTER.

LEAR.   Deny to speak with me! They are sick! They are weary! They have travell'd all the night! Mere fetches, the images of revolt and flying off. Fetch me a better answer.

GLOUCESTER.   My dear lord, you know the fiery quality of the duke; how unremovable and fix'd he is in his own course.

LEAR.   Vengeance! plague! death! confusion! fiery! what quality? Why, Gloucester, Gloucester, I'd speak with the Duke of Cornwall and his wife.

GLOUCESTER. Well, my good lord, I have inform'd them so.

LEAR. Inform'd them! Dost thou understand me, man?

GLOUCESTER. Ay, my good lord.

LEAR. The king would speak with Cornwall; the dear father would with his daughter speak, commands her service: are they inform'd of this? My breath and blood! Fiery! the fiery duke! Tell the hot duke that— No, but not yet; may be he is not well: infirmity doth still neglect all office whereto our health is bound; we are not ourselves when nature, being oppress'd, commands the mind to suffer with the body. I'll forbear; and am fall'n out with my more headier will, to take the indisposed and sickly fit for the sound man. Death on my state! wherefore [Looking on KENT] should he sit here? This act persuades me that this remotion of the duke and her is practice only. Give me my servant forth. Go tell the duke and 's wife I'd speak with them, now, presently: bid them come forth and hear me, or at their chamber door I'll beat the drum till it cry sleep to death.

GLOUCESTER. I would have all well betwixt you.   Exit.

LEAR. O me! my heart, my rising heart! but, down!

FOOL. Cry to it, nuncle, as the cockney did to the eels when she put 'em up i' the paste alive; she knapped 'em o' the coxcombs with a stick, and cried "Down, wantons, down!" 'Twas her brother that, in pure kindness to his horse, buttered his hay.

Re-enter GLOUCESTER, with CORNWALL, REGAN, and Servants.

LEAR. Good morrow to you both.

CORNWALL. Hail to your grace!

KENT is set at liberty.

REGAN. I am glad to see your highness.

LEAR. Regan, I think you are; I know what reason I have to think so: if thou shouldst not be glad, I would divorce me from thy mother's tomb, sepulchring an adult'ress. [To KENT] O! are you free? Some other time for that. Beloved Regan, thy sister's naught: O Regan! she hath tied sharp-tooth'd unkindness, like a vulture, here. [Points to his heart.] I can scarce speak to thee; thou 'lt not believe with how deprav'd a quality—O Regan!

REGAN. I pray you, sir, take patience. I have hope you less know how to value her desert than she to scant her duty.

LEAR. Say, how is that?

REGAN. I cannot think my sister in the least would fail her obligation: if, sir, perchance she have restrain'd the riots of your followers, 'tis on such ground, and to such wholesome end, as clears her from all blame.

LEAR. My curses on her!

REGAN. O, sir! you are old; nature in you stands on the very verge of her confine: you should be ruled and led by some discretion that discerns your state better than you yourself. Therefore I pray you that to our sister you do make return; say you have wrong'd her, sir.

LEAR. Ask her forgiveness? Do you but mark how this becomes the house: "Dear daughter, I confess that I am old; age is unnecessary: on my knees I beg [kneeling] that you'll vouchsafe me raiment, bed, and food."

REGAN. Good sir, no more; these are unsightly tricks. Return you to my sister.

LEAR [rising]. Never, Regan. She hath abated me of half my train; look'd black upon me; struck me with her tongue, most serpent-like, upon the very heart. All the stored vengeances of heaven fall on her ingrateful top! Strike her young bones, you taking airs, with lameness!

CORNWALL. Fie, sir, fie!

LEAR. You nimble lightnings, dart your blinding flames into her scornful eyes! Infect her beauty, you fen-suck'd fogs, drawn by the powerful sun, to fall and blast her pride!

REGAN.   O the blest gods! so will you wish on me, when the rash mood is on.

LEAR.   No, Regan, thou shalt never have my curse: thy tender-hefted nature shall not give thee o'er to harshness: her eyes are fierce, but thine do comfort and not burn. 'Tis not in thee to grudge my pleasures, to cut off my train, to bandy hasty words, to scant my sizes, and, in conclusion to oppose the bolt against my coming in: thou better know'st the offices of nature, bond of childhood, effects of courtesy, dues of gratitude; thy half o' the kingdom hast thou not forgot, wherein I thee endow'd.

REGAN.   Good sir, to the purpose.

LEAR.   Who put my man i' the stocks?   *Tucket within.*

CORNWALL.   What trumpet's that?

REGAN.   I know 't, my sister's: this approves her letter, that she would soon be here. [*Enter* OSWALD.] Is your lady come?

LEAR.   This is a slave, whose easy-borrow'd pride dwells in the fickle grace of her he follows. Out, varlet, from my sight!

CORNWALL.   What means your grace?

LEAR.   Who stock'd my servant? Regan, I have good hope thou didst not know on 't. Who comes here? [*Enter* GONERIL.] O heavens, if you do love old men, if your sweet sway allow obedience, if yourselves are old, make it your cause; send down and take my part! [*To* GONERIL] Art not ashamed to look upon this beard? O Regan! wilt thou take her by the hand?

GONERIL.   Why not by the hand, sir? How have I offended? All's not offense that indiscretion finds and dotage terms so.

LEAR.   O sides! you are too tough; will you yet hold? How came my man i' the stocks?

CORNWALL.   I set him there, sir; but his own disorders deserved much less advancement.

LEAR.   You! did you?

REGAN.   I pray you, father, being weak, seem so. If, till the expiration of your month, you will return and sojourn with my sister, dismissing half your train, come then to me: I am now from home, and out of that provision which shall be needful for your entertainment.

LEAR.   Return to her? and fifty men dismiss'd? No, rather I

abjure all roofs, and choose to wage against the enmity o' the air; to
be a comrade with the wolf and owl, necessity's sharp pinch! Return
with her! Why, the hot-blooded France, that dowerless took our
youngest born, I could as well be brought to knee his throne, and,

squire-like, pension beg to keep base life afoot. Return with her!
Persuade me rather to be slave and sumpter to this detested groom.

Pointing at OSWALD.

GONERIL. At your choice, sir.

LEAR. I prithee, daughter, do not make me mad: I will not
trouble thee, my child; farewell. We'll no more meet, no more see
one another; but yet thou art my flesh, my blood, my daughter; or
rather a disease that's in my flesh, which I must needs call mine: thou
art a boil, a plague-sore, an embossed carbuncle, in my corrupted
blood. But I'll not chide thee; let shame come when it will, I do not
call it: I do not bid the thunder-bearer shoot, nor tell tales of thee to
high-judging Jove. Mend when thou canst; be better at thy leisure: I
can be patient; I can stay with Regan, I and my hundred knights.

REGAN. Not altogether so: I look'd not for you yet, nor am
provided for your fit welcome. Give ear, sir, to my sister; for those
that mingle reason with your passion must be content to think you
old, and so— But she knows what she does.

LEAR.   Is this well spoken?

REGAN.   I dare avouch it, sir: what! fifty followers is it not well?
What should you need of more? Yea, or so many, sith that both
charge and danger speak 'gainst so great a number? How, in one
house, should many people, under two commands, hold amity? 'Tis
hard; almost impossible.

GONERIL.   Why might not you, my lord, receive attendance
from those that she calls servants, or from mine?

REGAN. Why not, my lord? If then they chanced to slack you we could control them. If you will come to me, for now I spy a danger, I entreat you to bring but five-and-twenty; to no more will I give place or notice.

LEAR. I gave you all—

REGAN. And in good time you gave it.

LEAR. Made you my guardians, my depositaries, but kept a reservation to be follow'd with such a number. What! must I come to you with five-and-twenty? Regan, said you so?

REGAN. And speak 't again, my lord; no more with me.

LEAR. Those wicked creatures yet do look well-favor'd when others are more wicked; not being the worst stands in some rank of praise. [To GONERIL] I'll go with thee: thy fifty yet doth double five-and-twenty, and thou art twice her love.

GONERIL. Hear me, my lord. What need you five-and-twenty, ten, or five, to follow in a house where twice so many have a command to tend you?

REGAN. What need one?

LEAR.   O! reason not the need; our basest beggars
Are in the poorest thing superfluous:
Allow not nature more than nature needs,
Man's life is cheap as beast's. Thou art a lady;
If only to go warm were gorgeous,
Why, nature needs not what thou gorgeous wear'st,
Which scarcely keeps thee warm. But, for true need—
You heavens, give me that patience, patience I need!
You see me here, you gods, a poor old man,
As full of grief as age; wretched in both!
If it be you that stirs these daughters' hearts
Against their father, fool me not so much
To bear it tamely; touch me with noble anger,
And let not women's weapons, water drops,
Stain my man's cheeks! No, you unnatural hags,
I will have such revenges on you both
That all the world shall—I will do such things,
What they are yet I know not, but they shall be
The terrors of the earth. You think I'll weep;
No, I'll not weep:
I have full cause of weeping, but this heart

Shall break into a hundred thousand flaws
Or ere I'll weep. O fool! I shall go mad.

Exeunt LEAR, GLOUCESTER, KENT, *and Fool.*

CORNWALL.   Let us withdraw, 'twill be a storm.

Storm heard at a distance.

REGAN.   This house is little: the old man and his people cannot
be well bestow'd.

GONERIL.   'Tis his own blame; hath put himself from rest, and must needs taste his folly.

REGAN.   For his particular, I'll receive him gladly, but not one follower.

GONERIL.   So am I purposed. Where is my Lord of Gloucester?

CORNWALL.   Follow'd the old man forth. He is return'd.

Re-enter GLOUCESTER.

GLOUCESTER.   The king is in high rage.

CORNWALL.   Whither is he going?

GLOUCESTER.   He calls to horse; but will I know not whither.

CORNWALL.   'Tis best to give him way; he leads himself.

GONERIL.   My lord, entreat him by no means to stay.

GLOUCESTER.   Alack! the night comes on, and the high winds do sorely ruffle; for many miles about there's scarce a bush.

REGAN.   O! sir, to wilful men, the injuries that they themselves procure must be their schoolmasters. Shut up your doors; he is attended with a desperate train, and what they may incense him to, being apt to have his ear abused, wisdom bids fear.

CORNWALL.   Shut up your doors, my lord; 'tis a wild night: my Regan counsels well: come out o' the storm.   *Exeunt.*

ACT THREE

SCENE I.   *A Heath.*

A storm, with thunder and lightning. Enter KENT *and a Gentleman, meeting.*

KENT.   Who's there, besides foul weather?

GENTLEMAN.   One minded like the weather, most unquietly.

KENT.   I know you. Where's the king?

GENTLEMAN.   Contending with the fretful elements; bids the wind blow the earth into the sea, or swell the curled waters 'bove the main, that things might change or cease; tears his white hair, which the impetuous blasts, with eyeless rage, catch in their fury, and make nothing of; strives in his little world of man to outscorn the to-and-fro-conflicting wind and rain. This night, wherein the cub-drawn bear would couch, the lion and the belly-pinched wolf keep their fur dry, unbonneted he runs, and bids what will take all.

KENT.   But who is with him?

GENTLEMAN.   None but the fool, who labors to outjest his heart-struck injuries.

KENT.   Sir, I do know you; and dare, upon the warrant of my note, commend a dear thing to you. There is division, although as yet the face of it be cover'd with mutual cunning, 'twixt Albany and Cornwall; who have—as who have not, that their great stars throned and set high?—servants, who seem no less, which are to France the spies and speculations intelligent of our state; what hath been seen, either in snuffs and packings of the dukes, or the hard rein which both of them have borne against the old kind king; or something deeper, whereof perchance these are but furnishings; but, true it is, from France there comes a power into this scatter'd kingdom; who already, wise in our negligence, have secret feet in some of our best ports, and are at point to show their open banner. Now to you: if on my credit you dare build so far to make your speed to Dover, you shall find some that will thank you, making just report of how unnatural and bemadding sorrow the king hath cause to plain. I am a gentleman of blood and breeding, and from some knowledge and assurance offer this office to you.

GENTLEMAN.   I will talk further with you.

KENT.   No, do not. For confirmation that I am much more than my out-wall, open this purse, and take what it contains. If you shall see Cordelia, as fear not but you shall, show her this ring, and she will tell you who your fellow is that yet you do not know. Fie on this storm! I will go seek the king.

GENTLEMAN.   Give me your hand. Have you no more to say?

KENT.   Few words, but, to effect, more than all yet; that, when we have found the king, in which your pain that way, I'll this, he that first lights on him holla the other.   *Exeunt severally.*

SCENE II.   *Another part of the Heath. Storm still.*

Enter LEAR *and Fool.*

LEAR.   Blow, winds, and crack your cheeks! rage! blow!
You cataracts and hurricanoes, spout
Till you have drench'd our steeples, drown'd the cocks!
You sulphurous and thought-executing fires,
Vaunt-couriers to oak-cleaving thunderbolts,
Singe my white head! And thou, all-shaking thunder,
Smite flat the thick rotundity o' the world!
Crack nature's moulds, all germens spill at once
That make ingrateful man!

FOOL.   O nuncle, court holy-water in a dry house is better than
this rainwater out o' door. Good nuncle, in, and ask thy daughters'
blessing; here's a night pities neither wise man nor fool.

LEAR.   Rumble thy bellyful! Spit, fire! spout, rain!
Nor rain, wind, thunder, fire, are my daughters:
I tax not you, you elements, with unkindness;
I never gave you kingdom, call'd you children,
You owe me no subscription: then let fall
Your horrible pleasure; here I stand, your slave,
A poor, infirm, weak, and despis'd old man.
But yet I call you servile ministers,
That have with two pernicious daughters join'd
Your high-engender'd battles 'gainst a head
So old and white as this. O! O! 'tis foul.

69

FOOL. He that has a house to put 's head in has a good headpiece.

> *The codpiece that will house*
> *Before the head has any,*
> *The head and he shall louse;*
> *So beggars marry many.*
> *The man that makes his toe*
> *What he his heart should make,*
> *Shall of a corn cry woe,*
> *And turn his sleep to wake.*

For there was never yet fair woman but she made mouths in a glass.

LEAR. No, I will be the pattern of all patience; I will say nothing.

Enter KENT.

KENT. Who's there?

FOOL. Marry, here's grace, and a codpiece; that's a wise man and a fool.

KENT. Alas! sir, are you here? things that love night love not such nights as these; the wrathful skies gallow the very wanderers of the dark, and make them keep their caves. Since I was man such sheets of fire, such bursts of horrid thunder, such groans of roaring wind and rain, I never remember to have heard; man's nature cannot carry the affliction nor the fear.

LEAR.   Let the great gods,
That keep this dreadful pudder o'er our heads,
Find out their enemies now. Tremble, thou wretch,
That hast within thee undivulged crimes,
Unwhipp'd of justice; hide thee, thou bloody hand,
Thou perjur'd, and thou simular of virtue
That art incestuous; caitiff, to pieces shake,
That under covert and convenient seeming
Hast practised on man's life; close pent-up guilts,
Rive your concealing continents, and cry
These dreadful summoners grace. I am a man
More sinn'd against than sinning.

KENT. Alack! bareheaded! Gracious my lord, hard by here is a hovel; some friendship will it lend you 'gainst the tempest; repose you there while I to this hard house—more harder than the stone whereof 'tis rais'd, which even but now, demanding after you, denied me to come in—return and force their scanted courtesy.

LEAR.   My wits begin to turn. Come on, my boy. How dost, my boy? Art cold? I am cold myself. Where is this straw, my fellow? The art of our necessities is strange, that can make vile things precious. Come, your hovel. Poor fool and knave, I have one part in my heart that's sorry yet for thee.

FOOL.   *He that has and a little tiny wit,*
         With hey, ho, the wind and the rain,
         Must make content with his fortunes fit,
         Though the rain it raineth every day.

LEAR.   True, my good boy. Come, bring us to this hovel.

Exeunt LEAR *and* KENT.

FOOL.   This is a brave night to cool a courtesan. I'll speak a prophecy ere I go:
         When priests are more in word than matter;
         When brewers mar their malt with water;
         When nobles are their tailors' tutors;
         No heretics burn'd, but wenches' suitors;
         When every case in law is right;
         No squire in debt, nor no poor knight;
         When slanders do not live in tongues;
         Nor cutpurses come not to throngs;
         When usurers tell their gold i' the field;
         And bawds and whores do churches build;
         Then shall the realm of Albion
         Come to great confusion:
         Then comes the time, who lives to see 't,
         That going shall be used with feet.
This prophecy Merlin shall make; for I live before his time.

Exit.

SCENE III.   *A Room in Gloucester's Castle.*

Enter GLOUCESTER *and* EDMUND.

GLOUCESTER.   Alack, alack! Edmund, I like not this unnatural
dealing. When I desired their leave that I might pity him, they took
from me the use of mine own house; charged me, on pain of their
perpetual displeasure, neither to speak of him, entreat for him, nor
any way sustain him.

EDMUND.   Most savage and unnatural!

GLOUCESTER.   Go to; say you nothing. There is division between the dukes, and a worse matter than that. I have received a
letter this night; 'tis dangerous to be spoken; I have locked the letter
in my closet. These injuries the king now bears will be revenged
home; there's part of a power already footed; we must incline to the
king. I will look him and privily relieve him; go you and maintain talk
with the duke, that my charity be not of him perceived. If he ask for
me, I am ill and gone to bed. If I die for it, as no less is threatened
me, the king, my old master, must be relieved. There is some strange
thing toward, Edmund; pray you, be careful.   *Exit.*

EDMUND.   This courtesy, forbid thee, shall the duke instantly
know; and of that letter too: this seems a fair deserving, and must
draw me that which my father loses; no less than all: the younger
rises when the old doth fall.   *Exit.*

SCENE IV. *The Heath. Before a Hovel.*

Enter LEAR, KENT, *and Fool.*

KENT. Here is the place, my lord; good my lord, enter: the tyranny of the open night's too rough for nature to endure.

Storm still.

LEAR. Let me alone.

KENT. Good my lord, enter here.

LEAR. Wilt break my heart?

KENT. I'd rather break mine own. Good my lord, enter.

LEAR. Thou think'st 'tis much that this contentious storm invades us to the skin: so 'tis to thee; but where the greater malady is fix'd, the lesser is scarce felt. Thou 'dst shun a bear; but if thy flight lay toward the roaring sea, thou 'dst meet the bear i' the mouth. When the mind's free the body's delicate; the tempest in my mind doth from my senses take all feeling else save what beats there. Filial ingratitude! Is it not as this mouth should tear this hand for lifting food to 't? But I will punish home: no, I will weep no more. In such a night to shut me out! Pour on; I will endure. In such a night as this! O Regan, Goneril! Your old kind father, whose frank heart gave all— O! that way madness lies; let me shun that; no more of that.

KENT. Good my lord, enter here.

LEAR. Prithee, go in thyself; seek thine own ease: this tempest will not give me leave to ponder on things would hurt me more. But

I'll go in. *[To the Fool]* In, boy; go first. You houseless poverty—
      Nay, get thee in. I'll pray, and then I'll sleep.

Fool goes in.

      Poor naked wretches, wheresoe'er you are,
      That bide the pelting of this pitiless storm,
      How shall your houseless heads and unfed sides,
      Your loop'd and window'd raggedness, defend you
      From seasons such as these? O! I have ta'en
      Too little care of this. Take physic, pomp;
      Expose thyself to feel what wretches feel,
      That thou mayst shake the superflux to them,
      And show the heavens more just.

EDGAR *[within].*   Fathom and half, fathom and half! Poor Tom!

The Fool runs out from the hovel.

FOOL.   Come not in here, nuncle; here's a spirit. Help me! help me!

KENT.   Give me thy hand. Who's there?

FOOL.   A spirit, a spirit: he says his name's poor Tom.

KENT.   What art thou that dost grumble there i' the straw? Come forth.

Enter EDGAR *disguised as a madman.*

EDGAR.   Away! the foul fiend follows me! Through the sharp hawthorn blow the winds. Humph! go to thy cold bed and warm thee.

LEAR.   Didst thou give all to thy two daughters? And art thou come to this?

EDGAR.   Who gives any thing to poor Tom? whom the foul fiend hath led through fire and through flame, through ford and whirlpool, o'er bog and quagmire; that hath laid knives under his pillow, and halters in his pew; set ratsbane by his porridge; made him proud of heart, to ride on a bay trotting horse over four-inched bridges, to course his own shadow for a traitor. Bless thy five wits! Tom's a-cold. O! do de, do de, do de. Bless thee from whirlwinds, star-blasting, and taking! Do poor Tom some charity, whom the foul fiend vexes. There could I have him now, and there, and there, and there again, and there.   *Storm still.*

LEAR.   What! have his daughters brought him to this pass?
Couldst thou save nothing? Didst thou give them all?

FOOL.   Nay, he reserved a blanket, else we had been all
shamed.

LEAR.   Now all the plagues that in the pendulous air hang fated
o'er men's faults light on thy daughters!

KENT.   He hath no daughters, sir.

LEAR.   Death, traitor! nothing could have subdued nature to
such a lowness but his unkind daughters. Is it the fashion that
discarded fathers should have thus little mercy on their flesh?
Judicious punishment! 'twas this flesh begot those pelican daughters.

EDGAR.   Pillicock sat on Pellicock's hill: halloo, halloo, loo, loo!

FOOL.   This cold night will turn us all to fools and madmen.

EDGAR.   Take heed o' the foul fiend. Obey thy parents; keep
thy word justly; swear not; commit not with man's sworn spouse; set
not thy sweet heart on proud array. Tom's a-cold.

LEAR.   What hast thou been?

EDGAR.   A servingman, proud in heart and mind; that curled
my hair, wore gloves in my cap, served the lust of my mistress' heart,
and did the act of darkness with her; swore as many oaths as I spake
words, and broke them in the sweet face of heaven; one that slept in
the contriving of lust, and waked to do it. Wine loved I deeply, dice
dearly, and in woman out-paramoured the Turk: false of heart, light
of ear, bloody of hand; hog in sloth, fox in stealth, wolf in greediness,
dog in madness, lion in prey. Let not the creaking of shoes nor the
rustling of silks betray thy poor heart to woman: keep thy foot out of
brothels, thy hand out of plackets, thy pen from lenders' books, and
defy the foul fiend. Still through the hawthorn blows the cold wind;
says suum, mun, hey no nonny. Dolphin my boy, my boy; sessa! let
him trot by.   *Storm still.*

LEAR.   Why, thou wert better in thy grave than to answer with
thy uncovered body this extremity of the skies. Is man no more than
this? Consider him well. Thou owest the worm no silk, the beast no
hide, the sheep no wool, the cat no perfume. Ha! here's three on 's
are sophisticated; thou art the thing itself; unaccommodated man is
no more but such a poor, bare, forked animal as thou art. Off, off, you
lendings! Come; unbutton here.   *Tearing off his clothes.*

FOOL.   Prithee, nuncle, be contented; 'tis a naughty night to swim in. Now a little fire in a wild field were like an old lecher's heart; a small spark, all the rest on 's body cold. Look! here comes a walking fire.

Enter GLOUCESTER, *with a torch.*

EDGAR.   This is the foul fiend Flibbertigibbet: he begins at curfew, and walks till the first cock; he gives the web and the pin, squints the eye, and makes the harelip; mildews the white wheat, and hurts the poor creature of earth.

> *Swithold footed thrice the old;*
> *He met the nightmare, and her nine fold;*
> *Bid her alight,*
> *And her troth-plight,*
> *And aroint thee, witch, aroint thee!*

KENT.   How fares your grace?

LEAR.   What's he?

KENT.   Who's there? What is 't you seek?

GLOUCESTER.   What are you there? Your names?

EDGAR.   Poor Tom; that eats the swimming frog, the toad, the tadpole, the wall-newt, and the water; that in the fury of his heart, when the foul fiend rages, eats cow-dung for sallets; swallows the old

rat and the ditch-dog; drinks the green mantle of the standing pool; who is whipped from tithing to tithing, and stock-punished, and imprisoned; who hath had three suits to his back, six shirts to his body,

> Horse to ride, and weapon to wear,
> But mice and rats and such small deer,
> Have been Tom's food for seven long year.

Beware my follower. Peace, Smulkin! peace, thou fiend!

GLOUCESTER. What! hath your grace no better company?

EDGAR. The prince of darkness is a gentleman; Modo he's call'd, and Mahu.

GLOUCESTER. Our flesh and blood, my lord, is grown so vile, that it doth hate what gets it.

EDGAR. Poor Tom's a-cold.

GLOUCESTER.

> Go in with me. My duty cannot suffer
> To obey in all your daughters' hard commands:
> Though their injunction be to bar my doors,
> And let this tyrannous night take hold upon you,
> Yet have I ventured to come seek you out
> And bring you where both fire and food is ready.

LEAR. First let me talk with this philosopher. What is the cause
of thunder?

KENT. Good my lord, take his offer; go into the house.

LEAR. I'll talk a word with this same learned Theban. What is
your study?

EDGAR. How to prevent the fiend, and to kill vermin.

LEAR. Let me ask you one word in private.

KENT. Importune him once more to go, my lord; his wits begin
to unsettle.

GLOUCESTER. Canst thou blame him? *[Storm still]* His daughters seek his death. Ah! that good Kent; he said it would be thus,
poor banish'd man! Thou say'st the king grows mad; I'll tell thee,
friend, I am almost mad myself. I had a son, now outlaw'd from my
blood; he sought my life, but lately, very late; I lov'd him, friend, no
father his son dearer; true to tell thee, the grief hath crazed my wits.
What a night 's this I do beseech your grace—

LEAR. O! cry you mercy, sir. Noble philosopher, your company.

EDGAR. Tom's a-cold.

GLOUCESTER. In, fellow, there, into the hovel: keep thee warm.

LEAR. Come, let's in all.

KENT. This way, my lord.

LEAR. With him; I will keep still with my philosopher.

KENT. Good my lord, soothe him; let him take the fellow.

GLOUCESTER. Take him you on.

KENT. Sirrah, come on; go along with us.

LEAR. Come, good Athenian.

GLOUCESTER. No words, no words: hush.

EDGAR.   *Child Rowland to the dark tower came,*
              His word was still, Fie, foh, and fum,
              I smell the blood of a British man.

Exeunt.

SCENE V.   *A Room in Gloucester's Castle.*

Enter CORNWALL *and* EDMUND.

CORNWALL. I will have my revenge ere I depart this house.

EDMUND. How, my lord, I may be censured, that nature thus gives way to loyalty, something fears me to think of.

CORNWALL. I now perceive it was not altogether your brother's evil disposition made him seek his death; but a provoking merit, set a-work by a reproveable badness in himself.

EDMUND. How malicious is my fortune, that I must repent to be just! This is the letter he spoke of, which approves him an intelligent party to the advantages of France. O heavens! that this treason were not, or not I the detector!

CORNWALL. Go with me to the duchess.

EDMUND. If the matter of this paper be certain, you have mighty business in hand.

CORNWALL. True or false, it hath made thee Earl of Gloucester. Seek out where thy father is, that he may be ready for our apprehension.

EDMUND [*aside*]. If I find him comforting the king, it will stuff his suspicion more fully. I will persevere in my course of loyalty, though the conflict be sore between that and my blood.

CORNWALL. I will lay trust upon thee; and thou shalt find a dearer father in my love.   *Exeunt.*

80

SCENE VI.   *A Chamber in a Farmhouse adjoining the Castle.*

Enter GLOUCESTER, LEAR, KENT, *Fool, and* EDGAR.

GLOUCESTER.   Here is better than the open air; take it thankfully. I will piece out the comfort with what addition I can: I will not be long from you.

KENT.   All the power of his wits have given way to his impatience. The gods reward your kindness!

Exit GLOUCESTER.

EDGAR.   Frateretto calls me, and tells me Nero is an angler in the lake of darkness. Pray, innocent, and beware the foul fiend.

FOOL.   Prithee, nuncle, tell me whether a madman be a gentleman or a yeoman?

LEAR.   A king, a king!

FOOL.   No; he's a yeoman that has a gentleman to his son; for he's a mad yeoman that sees his son a gentleman before him.

LEAR.   To have a thousand with red burning spits come hissing in upon 'em—

EDGAR.   The foul fiend bites my back.

FOOL.   He's mad that trusts in the tameness of a wolf, a horse's health, a boy's love, or a whore's oath.

LEAR.   It shall be done; I will arraign them straight. [*To* EDGAR] Come, sit thou here, most learned justicer. [*To the Fool*] Thou, sapient sir, sit here. Now, you she foxes!

81

EDGAR.   Look where he stands and glares! Wantest thou eyes at
trial, madam?

FOOL [sings].

> Come o'er the bourn, Bessy, to me—
> Her boat hath a leak,
> And she must not speak
> Why she dares not come over to thee.

EDGAR.   The foul fiend haunts poor Tom in the voice of a
nightingale. Hoppedance cries in Tom's belly for two white herring.
Croak not, black angel; I have no food for thee.

KENT.   How do you, sir? Stand you not so amazed: will you lie
down and rest upon the cushions?

LEAR.   I'll see their trial first. Bring in their evidence. [To
EDGAR] Thou robed man of justice, take thy place. [To the Fool] And
thou, his yokefellow of equity, bench by his side. [To KENT] You are o'
the commission, sit you too.

EDGAR.   Let us deal justly.

> Sleepest or wakest thou, jolly shepherd?
> Thy sheep be in the corn;
> And for one blast of thy minikin mouth,
> Thy sheep shall take no harm.

Purr! the cat is gray.

LEAR.   Arraign her first; 'tis Goneril. I here take my oath before
this honorable assembly, she kicked the poor king her father.

FOOL.   Come hither, mistress. Is your name Goneril?

LEAR.   She cannot deny it.

FOOL.   Cry you mercy, I took you for a joint-stool.

LEAR.   And here's another, whose warp'd looks proclaim what
store her heart is made on. Stop her there! Arms, arms, sword, fire!
Corruption in the place! False justicer, why hast thou let her 'scape?

EDGAR.   Bless thy five wits!

KENT.   O pity! Sir, where is the patience now that you so oft
have boasted to retain?

EDGAR [aside].   My tears begin to take his part so much, they'll
mar my counterfeiting.

LEAR.   The little dogs and all, Tray, Blanch, and Sweetheart,
see, they bark at me.

EDGAR.   Tom will throw his head at them. Avaunt, you curs!

> Be thy mouth or black or white,
> Tooth that poisons if it bite;

Mastiff, greyhound, mongrel grim,
  Hound or spaniel, brach or lym;
Or bobtail tike or trundle-tail;
  Tom will make them weep and wail:
For, with throwing thus my head,
  Dogs leap the hatch, and all are fed.

Do de, de, de. Sessa! Come, march to wakes and fairs and market towns. Poor Tom, thy horn is dry.

    LEAR.   Then let them anatomize Regan, see what breeds about her heart. Is there any cause in nature that makes these hard hearts? [*To* EDGAR] You, sir, I entertain for one of my hundred; only I do not like the fashion of your garments: you will say they are Persian attire; but let them be changed.

    KENT.   Now, good my lord, lie here and rest awhile.

    LEAR.   Make no noise, make no noise; draw the curtains: so, so, so. We'll go to supper i' the morning: so, so, so.

    FOOL.   And I'll go to bed at noon.

Re-enter GLOUCESTER.

GLOUCESTER. Come hither, friend: where is the king my master?

KENT. Here, sir; but trouble him not, his wits are gone.

GLOUCESTER. Good friend, I prithee, take him in thy arms; I have o'erheard a plot of death upon him. There is a litter ready; lay him in 't, and drive toward Dover, friend, where thou shalt meet both welcome and protection. Take up thy master: if thou should'st dally half an hour, his life, with thine, and all that offer to defend him, stand in assured loss. Take up, take up; and follow me, that will to some provision give thee quick conduct.

KENT. Oppress'd nature sleeps: this rest might yet have balm'd thy broken sinews which, if convenience will not allow, stand in hard cure. *[To the Fool]* Come, help to bear thy master; thou must not stay behind.

GLOUCESTER.   Come, come, away.

Exeunt KENT, GLOUCESTER, *and the Fool, bearing off the King.*

EDGAR.   When we our betters see bearing our woes, we scarcely think our miseries our foes. Who alone suffers suffers most i' the mind, leaving free things and happy shows behind; but then the mind much sufferance doth o'erskip, when grief hath mates, and bearing fellowship. How light and portable my pain seems now, when that which makes me bend makes the king bow; he childed as I father'd! Tom, away! Mark the high noises, and thyself bewray when false opinion, whose wrong thought defiles thee, in thy just proof repeals and reconciles thee. What will hap more tonight, safe 'scape the king! Lurk, lurk.   *Exit.*

SCENE VII.   *A Room in Gloucester's Castle.*

Enter CORNWALL, REGAN, GONERIL, EDMUND, *and Servants.*

CORNWALL [*to* GONERIL].   Post speedily to my lord your husband; show him this letter: the army of France is landed. Seek out the traitor Gloucester.   *Exeunt some of the Servants.*

REGAN.　Hang him instantly.

GONERIL.　Pluck out his eyes.

CORNWALL.　Leave him to my displeasure. Edmund, keep you our sister company: the revenges we are bound to take upon your traitorous father are not fit for your beholding. Advise the duke, where you are going, to a most festinate preparation: we are bound to the like. Our posts shall be swift and intelligent betwixt us. Farewell, dear sister; farewell, my Lord of Gloucester. [*Enter* OSWALD] How now! where's the king?

OSWALD.　My Lord of Gloucester hath convey'd him hence: some five or six and thirty of his knights, hot questrists after him, met him at gate; who, with some other of the lord's dependants, are gone with him towards Dover, where they boast to have well-armed friends.

CORNWALL.　Get horses for your mistress.

GONERIL.　Farewell, sweet lord, and sister.

CORNWALL.　Edmund, farewell. [*Exeunt* GONERIL, EDMUND, *and* OSWALD]

Go seek the traitor Gloucester,
Pinion him like a thief, bring him before us.

[Exeunt other Servants.]

Though well we may not pass upon his life
Without the form of justice, yet our power
Shall do a court'sy to our wrath, which men
May blame but not control.
Who's there? The traitor?

Re-enter Servants, with GLOUCESTER *prisoner.*

REGAN.   Ingrateful fox! 'tis he.

CORNWALL.   Bind fast his corky arms.

GLOUCESTER.   What mean your graces? Good my friends, consider you are my guests: do me no foul play, friends.

CORNWALL.   Bind him, I say.   *Servants bind him.*

REGAN.   Hard, hard. O filthy traitor!

GLOUCESTER.   Unmerciful lady as you are, I'm none.

CORNWALL.   To this chair bind him. Villain, thou shalt find—

                    REGAN *plucks his beard.*

GLOUCESTER.   By the kind gods, 'tis most ignobly done to pluck me by the beard.

REGAN.   So white, and such a traitor!

GLOUCESTER.   Naughty lady, these hairs, which thou dost ravish from my chin, will quicken, and accuse thee: I am your host: with robbers' hands my hospitable favors you should not ruffle thus. What will you do?

CORNWALL.   Come, sir, what letters had you late from France?

REGAN.   Be simple-answer'd, for we know the truth.

CORNWALL.   And what confederacy have you with the traitors late footed in the kingdom?

REGAN.   To whose hands have you sent the lunatic king? Speak.

GLOUCESTER.   I have a letter guessingly set down, which came from one that's of a neutral heart, and not from one opposed.

CORNWALL.   Cunning.

REGAN.   And false.

CORNWALL.   Where hast thou sent the king?

GLOUCESTER.   To Dover.

REGAN.   Wherefore to Dover? Wast thou not charged at peril—

CORNWALL.   Wherefore to Dover? Let him answer that.

GLOUCESTER. I am tied to the stake, and I must stand the course.

REGAN. Wherefore to Dover?

GLOUCESTER.

> Because I would not see thy cruel nails
> Pluck out his poor old eyes; nor thy fierce sister
> In his anointed flesh stick boarish fangs.
> The sea, with such a storm as his bare head
> In hell-black night endured, would have buoy'd up,
> And quench'd the stelled fires;
> Yet, poor old heart, he holp the heavens to rain.
> If wolves had at thy gate howl'd that dearn time,
> Thou should'st have said "Good porter, turn the key."
> All cruels else subscribe: but I shall see
> The winged vengeance overtake such children.

CORNWALL. See 't shalt thou never. Fellows, hold the chair. Upon these eyes of thine I'll set my foot.

GLOUCESTER.   He that will think to live till he be old, give me some help! O cruel! O ye gods!

REGAN.   One side will mock another; the other too.

CORNWALL.   If you see vengeance—

FIRST SERVANT.

Hold your hand, my lord.
I have served you ever since I was a child,
But better service have I never done you
Than now to bid you hold.

REGAN.   How now, you dog!

FIRST SERVANT.   If you did wear a beard upon your chin I'd shake it on this quarrel. What do you mean?

CORNWALL.   My villain!   *They draw and fight.*
    FIRST SERVANT.   Nay then, come on, and take the chance of
anger.
    REGAN.   Give me thy sword. A peasant stand up thus!

Takes a sword and runs at him behind.
FIRST SERVANT.   O! I am slain. My lord, you have one eye left to
see some mischief on him. O!   *Dies.*

CORNWALL.   Lest it see more, prevent it. Out, vile jelly! Where is thy lustre now?

GLOUCESTER.   All dark and comfortless. Where's my son Edmund? Edmund, enkindle all the sparks of nature to quit this horrid act.

REGAN.   Out, treacherous villain! Thou call'st on him that hates thee; it was he that made the overture of thy treasons to us, who is too good to pity thee.

GLOUCESTER.   O my follies! Then Edgar was abused. Kind gods, forgive me that, and prosper him!

REGAN.   Go thrust him out at gates, and let him smell his way to Dover. [*Exit one with* GLOUCESTER.] How is 't, my lord? How look you?

CORNWALL.   I have receiv'd a hurt. Follow me, lady. Turn out that eyeless villain; throw this slave upon the dunghill. Regan, I

bleed apace: untimely comes this hurt. Give me your arm.

Exit CORNWALL, *led by* REGAN.

SECOND SERVANT.   I'll never care what wickedness I do if this
man come to good.

THIRD SERVANT.   If she live long, and in the end meet the old
course of death, women will all turn monsters.

SECOND SERVANT.

Let's follow the old earl, and get the Bedlam
To lead him where he would: his roguish madness
Allows itself to anything.

THIRD SERVANT.

Go thou; I'll fetch some flax and whites of eggs
To apply to his bleeding face. Now, heaven help him!

Exeunt severally.

ACT FOUR

SCENE I. *The Heath.*

Enter EDGAR.

EDGAR.   Yet better thus, and known to be contemn'd, than still contemn'd and flatter'd. To be worst, the lowest and most dejected thing of fortune, stands still in esperance, lives not in fear: the lamentable change is from the best; the worst returns to laughter. Welcome, then, thou unsubstantial air that I embrace: the wretch that thou hast blown unto the worst owes nothing to thy blasts. But who comes here? [*Enter* GLOUCESTER, *led by an old Man*] My father, poorly led? World, world, O world! But that thy strange mutations make us hate thee, life would not yield to age.

OLD MAN.   O my good lord! I have been your tenant, and your father's tenant, these fourscore years.

GLOUCESTER.   Away, get thee away; good friend, be gone: thy comforts can do me no good at all; thee they may hurt.

OLD MAN.   You cannot see your way.

GLOUCESTER.

> I have no way, and therefore want no eyes;
> I stumbled when I saw. Full oft 'tis seen,
> Our means secure us, and our mere defects
> Prove our commodities. Ah! dear son Edgar,
> The food of thy abused father's wrath;

Might I but live to see thee in my touch,
I'd say I had eyes again.

OLD MAN. How now! Who's there?

EDGAR [aside]. O gods! Who is 't can say "I am at the worst"? I am worse than e'er I was.

OLD MAN. 'Tis poor mad Tom.

EDGAR [aside]. And worse I may be yet; the worst is not so long as we can say "This is the worst."

OLD MAN. Fellow, where goest?

GLOUCESTER. Is it a beggarman?

OLD MAN. Madman and beggar too.

GLOUCESTER. He has some reason, else he could not beg. I' the last night's storm I such a fellow saw, which made me think a man a worm: my son came then into my mind; and yet my mind was then scarce friends with him: I have heard more since. As flies to wanton boys, are we to the gods; they kill us for their sport.

EDGAR [aside]. How should this be? Bad is the trade that must play fool to sorrow, angering itself and others. Bless thee, master!

GLOUCESTER. Is that the naked fellow?

OLD MAN. Ay, my lord.

GLOUCESTER. Then, prithee, get thee gone. If, for my sake, thou wilt o'ertake us, hence a mile or twain, i' the way toward Dover, do it for ancient love; and bring some covering for this naked soul, who I'll entreat to lead me.

OLD MAN. Alack, sir! he is mad.

GLOUCESTER. 'Tis the times' plague, when madmen lead the blind. Do as I bid thee, or rather do thy pleasure; above the rest, be gone.

OLD MAN. I'll bring him the best 'parel that I have, come on 't what will. *Exit.*

GLOUCESTER. Sirrah, naked fellow—

EDGAR. Poor Tom's a-cold. [Aside] I cannot daub it further.

GLOUCESTER. Come hither, fellow.

EDGAR [aside]. And yet I must. Bless thy sweet eyes, they bleed.

GLOUCESTER. Know'st thou the way to Dover?

EDGAR. Both stile and gate, horseway and footpath. Poor Tom hath been scared out of his good wits: bless thee, good man's son, from the foul fiend! Five fiends have been in poor Tom at once; of lust, as Obidicut; Hoberdidance, prince of dumbness; Mahu, of stealing; Modo, of murder; Flibbertigibbet, of mopping and mowing; who since possesses chambermaids and waiting women. So, bless thee, master!

GLOUCESTER. Here, take this purse, thou whom the heavens plagues have humbled to all strokes: that I am wretched makes thee the happier: heavens, deal so still! Let the superfluous and lust-dieted man, that slaves your ordinance, that will not see because he doth not feel, feel your power quickly; so distribution should undo excess, and each man have enough. Dost thou know Dover?

EDGAR. Ay, master.

GLOUCESTER. There is a cliff, whose high and bending head looks fearfully in the confined deep; bring me but to the very brim of it, and I'll repair the misery thou dost bear with something rich about me; from that place I shall no leading need.

EDGAR. Give me thy arm: poor Tom shall lead thee. *Exeunt.*

SCENE II.   *Before the Duke of Albany's Palace.*

Enter GONERIL *and* EDMUND.

GONERIL.   Welcome, my lord; I marvel our mild husband not met us on the way. [*Enter* OSWALD] Now, where's your master?

OSWALD.   Madam, within; but never man so changed. I told him of the army that was landed; he smiled at it: I told him you were coming; his answer was "The worse": of Gloucester's treachery, and of the loyal service of his son, when I inform'd him, then he call'd me sot, and told me I had turn'd the wrong side out: what most he should dislike seems pleasant to him; what like, offensive.

GONERIL [*to* EDMUND].   Then shall you go no further. It is the cowish terror of his spirit that dares not undertake; he'll not feel wrongs which tie him to an answer. Our wishes on the way may prove effects. Back, Edmund, to my brother; hasten his musters and conduct his powers: I must change arms at home, and give the distaff into my husband's hands. This trusty servant shall pass between us; ere long you are like to hear, if you dare venture in your own behalf, a mistress's command. Wear this; spare speech; [*giving a favor*] decline your head: this kiss, if it durst speak, would stretch thy spirits up into the air. Conceive, and fare thee well.

EDMUND.   Yours in the ranks of death.

GONERIL. My most dear Gloucester! [*Exit* EDMUND] O! the difference of man and man. To thee a woman's services are due: my fool usurps my body.

OSWALD. Madam, here comes my lord.   *Exit.*

Enter ALBANY.

GONERIL. I have been worth the whistle.

ALBANY. O Goneril!
You are not worth the dust which the rude wind
Blows in your face. I fear your disposition:
That nature, which contemns its origin,
Cannot be border'd certain in itself;
She that herself will sliver and disbranch
From her material sap, perforce must wither
And come to deadly use.

GONERIL. No more; the text is foolish.

ALBANY.   Wisdom and goodness to the vile seem vile;
Filths savor but themselves. What have you done?
Tigers, not daughters, what have you perform'd?
A father, and a gracious aged man,
Whose reverence the head-lugg'd bear would lick,
Most barbarous, most degenerate! have you madded.
Could my good brother suffer you to do it?
A man, a prince, by him so benefited!
If that the heavens do not their visible spirits
Send quickly down to tame these vile offenses,
It will come,
Humanity must perforce prey on itself,
Like monsters of the deep.

GONERIL. Milk-liver'd man! that bear'st a cheek for blows, a head for wrongs; who hast not in thy brows an eye discerning thine honor from thy suffering; that not know'st fools do those villains pity who are punish'd ere they have done their mischief. Where's thy drum? France spreads his banners in our noiseless land, with plumed helm thy slayer begins threats, whiles thou, a moral fool, sitt'st still, and criest "Alack! why does he so?"

ALBANY. See thyself, devil! Proper deformity seems not in the fiend so horrid as in woman.

GONERIL. O vain fool!

ALBANY. Thou changed and self-cover'd thing, for shame, bemonster not thy feature. Were 't my fitness to let these hands obey my blood, they are apt enough to dislocate and tear thy flesh and bones; howe'er thou art a fiend, a woman's shape doth shield thee.

GONERIL. Marry, your manhood—mew!

Enter a Messenger.

ALBANY. What news?

MESSENGER. O! my good lord, the Duke of Cornwall's dead; slain by his servant, going to put out the other eye of Gloucester.

ALBANY. Gloucester's eyes!

MESSENGER. A servant that he bred, thrill'd with remorse, oppos'd against the act, bending his sword to his great master; who, thereat enrag'd, flew on him, and amongst them fell'd him dead; but not without that harmful stroke, which since hath pluck'd him after.

ALBANY.   This shows you are above,
    You justicers, that these our nether crimes
    So speedily can venge! But, O poor Gloucester!
    Lost he his other eye?

MESSENGER. Both, both, my lord. This letter, madam, craves a
speedy answer; 'tis from your sister.   *Presents a letter.*

GONERIL *[aside].* One way I like this well; but being widow,
and my Gloucester with her, may all the building in my fancy pluck
upon my hateful life: another way, the news is not so tart. I'll read,
and answer.   *Exit.*

ALBANY. Where was his son when they did take his eyes?

MESSENGER. Come with my lady hither.

ALBANY. He is not here.

MESSENGER. No, my good lord; I met him back again.

ALBANY. Knows he the wickedness?

MESSENGER. Ay, my good lord; 'twas he inform'd against him,
and quit the house on purpose that their punishment might have the
freer course.

ALBANY.   Gloucester, I live
           To thank thee for the love thou show'dst the king,
           And to revenge thine eyes. Come hither, friend:
           Tell me what more thou knowest.   *Exeunt.*

SCENE III.   *The French Camp near Dover.*

Enter KENT *and a Gentleman.*

KENT.   Why the King of France is so suddenly gone back know
you the reason?

GENTLEMAN.   Something he left imperfect in the state, which
since his coming forth is thought of; which imports to the kingdom so
much fear and danger that his personal return was most required and
necessary.

KENT.   Who hath he left behind him general?

GENTLEMAN.   The Marshal of France, Monsieur La Far.

KENT.   Did your letters pierce the queen to any demonstration
of grief?

GENTLEMAN.   Ay, sir; she took them, read them in my presence;
and now and then an ample tear trill'd down her delicate cheek; it
seem'd she was a queen over her passion; who, most rebel-like,
sought to be king o'er her.

KENT.   O! then it mov'd her.

GENTLEMAN.

        Not to a rage; patience and sorrow strove
        Who should express her goodliest. You have seen
        Sunshine and rain at once; her smiles and tears
        Were like a better way; those happy smilets

That play'd on her ripe lip seem'd not to know
What guests were in her eyes; which parted thence,
As pearls from diamonds dropp'd. In brief,
Sorrow would be a rarity most belov'd,
If all could so become it.

KENT.   Made she no verbal question?

GENTLEMAN.

Faith, once or twice she heaved the name of "father"
Pantingly forth, as if it press'd her heart;
Cried "Sisters! sisters! Shame of ladies! sisters!
Kent! father! sisters! What? i' the storm? i' the night?
Let pity not be believed!" There she shook
The holy water from her heavenly eyes,
And clamor-moisten'd, then away she started
To deal with grief alone.

KENT.   It is the stars, the stars above us, govern our conditions;
else one self mate and make could not beget such different issues.
You spoke not with her since?

GENTLEMAN.   No.

KENT.   Was this before the king return'd?

GENTLEMAN.   No, since.

KENT.   Well, sir, the poor distressed Lear's i' the town; who
sometime, in his better tune, remembers what we are come about,
and by no means will yield to see his daughter.

GENTLEMAN.   Why, good sir?

KENT.   A sovereign shame so elbows him: his own unkindness,
that stripp'd her from his benediction, turn'd her to foreign
casualties, gave her dear rights to his dog-hearted daughters, these
things sting his mind so venomously that burning shame detains him
from Cordelia.

GENTLEMAN.   Alack! poor gentleman.

KENT.   Of Albany's and Cornwall's powers you heard not?

GENTLEMAN.   'Tis so, they are afoot.

KENT.   Well, sir, I'll bring you to our master Lear, and leave
you to attend him. Some dear cause will in concealment wrap me up
awhile; when I am known aright, you shall not grieve lending me this
acquaintance. I pray you, go along with me.   *Exeunt.*

SCENE IV. *The Same. A Tent.*

Enter, with drum and colors, CORDELIA, *Doctor, and Soldiers.*

CORDELIA.   Alack! 'tis he: why, he was met even now as mad as the vex'd sea; singing aloud; crown'd with rank fumiter and furrow weeds, with hordocks, hemlock, nettles, cuckoo flowers, darnel, and all the idle weeds that grow in our sustaining corn. A sentry send forth; search every acre in the high-grown field, and bring him to our eye. *[Exit an Officer.]* What can man's wisdom in the restoring his bereaved sense? He that helps him take all my outward worth.

DOCTOR.   There is means, madam; our foster nurse of nature is repose, the which he lacks; that to provoke in him, are many simples operative, whose power will close the eye of anguish.

CORDELIA.   All bless'd secrets, all you unpublish'd virtues of the earth, spring with my tears! be aidant and remediate in the good man's distress! Seek, seek for him, lest his ungovern'd rage dissolve the life that wants the means to lead it.

Enter a Messenger.

MESSENGER.   News, madam; the British powers are marching hitherward.

CORDELIA.   'Tis known before; our preparation stands in expec-

tation of them. O dear father! It is thy business that I go about; therefore great France my mourning and important tears hath pitied. No blown ambition doth our arms incite, but love, dear love, and our aged father's right. Soon may I hear and see him!   *Exeunt.*

SCENE V.   *A Room in Gloucester's Castle.*

Enter REGAN *and* OSWALD.

REGAN.   But are my brother's powers set forth?

OSWALD.   Ay, madam.

REGAN.   Himself in person there?

OSWALD.   Madam, with much ado: your sister is the better soldier.

REGAN.   Lord Edmund spake not with your lord at home?

OSWALD.   No, madam.

REGAN.   What might import my sister's letter to him?

OSWALD.   I know not, lady.

REGAN.   Faith, he is posted hence on serious matter. It was great ignorance, Gloucester's eyes being out, to let him live; where he arrives he moves all hearts against us. Edmund, I think, is gone, in pity of his misery, to dispatch his nighted life; moreover, to descry the strength o' th' enemy.

OSWALD.   I must needs after him, madam, with my letter.

REGAN.   Our troops set forth to-morrow; stay with us, the ways are dangerous.

OSWALD.   I may not, madam; my lady charged my duty in this business.

REGAN.   Why should she write to Edmund? Might not you transport her purposes by word? Belike, something—I know not what. I'll love thee much, let me unseal the letter.

OSWALD.   Madam, I had rather—

REGAN.   I know your lady does not love her husband; I am sure of that: and at her late being here she gave strange œilliads and most speaking looks to noble Edmund. I know you are of her bosom.

OSWALD.   I, madam!

REGAN.   I speak in understanding; you are, I know't:
                Therefore I do advise you, take this note:
                My lord is dead; Edmund and I have talk'd
                And more convenient is he for my hand
                Than for your lady's. You may gather more.
                If you do find him, pray you give him this,
                And when your mistress hears thus much from you,
                I pray desire her call her wisdom to her:
                So, fare you well.
                If you do chance to hear of that blind traitor,
                Preferment falls on him that cuts him off.

OSWALD.   Would I could meet him, madam: I would show what party I do follow.

REGAN.   Fare thee well.   *Exeunt.*

SCENE VI.   *The Country near Dover.*

Enter GLOUCESTER *and* EDGAR *dressed like a peasant.*

GLOUCESTER.   When shall we come to the top of that same hill?

EDGAR.   You do climb up it now; look how we labor.

GLOUCESTER.   Methinks the ground is even.

EDGAR.   Horrible steep: Hark! do you hear the sea?

GLOUCESTER.   No, truly.

EDGAR.   Why, then your other senses grow imperfect by your
eyes' anguish.

GLOUCESTER.   So may it be, indeed. Methinks thy voice is
alter'd, and thou speak'st in better phrase and matter than thou
didst.

EDGAR.   You're much deceiv'd; in nothing am I changed but in
my garments.

GLOUCESTER.   Methinks you're better spoken.

EDGAR.   Come on, sir; here's the place: stand still. How fearful
and dizzy 'tis to cast one's eyes so low! The crows and choughs that
wing the midway air show scarce so gross as beetles; halfway down
hangs one that gathers sampire, dreadful trade! Methinks he seems
no bigger than his head. The fishermen that walk upon the beach
appear like mice, and yond tall anchoring bark diminish'd to her
cock, her cock a buoy almost too small for sight. The murmuring
surge, that on the unnumber'd idle pebbles chafes, cannot be heard
so high. I'll look no more, lest my brain turn, and the deficient sight
topple down headlong.

GLOUCESTER.   Set me where you stand.

EDGAR. Give me your hand; you are now within a foot of the extreme verge: for all beneath the moon would I not leap upright.

GLOUCESTER. Let go my hand. Here, friend, 's another purse; in it a jewel well worth a poor man's taking: fairies and gods prosper it with thee! Go thou further off; bid me farewell, and let me hear thee going.

EDGAR. Now fare you well, good sir.

GLOUCESTER. With all my heart.

EDGAR. Why I do trifle thus with his despair is done to cure it.

GLOUCESTER [*kneeling*]. O you mighty gods! This world I do renounce, and in your sights shake patiently my great affliction off; if I could bear it longer, and not fall to quarrel with your great opposeless wills, my snuff and loathed part of nature should burn itself out. If Edgar live, O, bless him! Now, fellow, fare thee well.

He throws himself forward and falls.

EDGAR. Gone, sir: farewell. And yet I know not how conceit may rob the treasury of life when life itself yields to the theft; had he been where he thought by this had thought been past. Alive or dead?

Ho, you sir! friend! Hear you, sir! speak! Thus might he pass indeed;
yet he revives. What are you, sir?

GLOUCESTER.   Away and let me die.

EDGAR.   Hadst thou been aught but gossamer, feathers, air, so
many fathom down precipitating, thou 'dst shiver'd like an egg; but
thou dost breathe, hast heavy substance, bleed'st not, speak'st, art
sound. Ten masts at each make not the altitude which thou hast
perpendicularly fell: thy life's a miracle. Speak yet again.

GLOUCESTER.   But have I fallen or no?

EDGAR.   From the dread summit of this chalky bourn. Look up
a-height; the shrill-gorged lark so far cannot be seen or heard: do but
look up.

GLOUCESTER.   Alack! I have no eyes. Is wretchedness deprived
that benefit to end itself by death? 'Twas yet some comfort, When
misery could beguile the tyrant's rage, and frustrate his proud will.

EDGAR.   Give me your arm: up: so; how is 't? Feel you your
legs? You stand.

GLOUCESTER.   Too well, too well.

EDGAR.   This is above all strangeness. Upon the crown o' the
cliff what thing was that which parted from you?

GLOUCESTER.   A poor unfortunate beggar.

EDGAR.   As I stood here below methought his eyes were two
full moons; he had a thousand noses, horns whelk'd and wav'd like
the enridged sea: it was some fiend; therefore, thou happy father,
think that the clearest gods, who make them honors of men's
impossibilities, have preserved thee.

GLOUCESTER.   I do remember now; henceforth I'll bear affliction till it do cry out itself, "Enough, enough," and die. That thing

you speak of, I took it for a man; often 'twould say "The fiend, the fiend": he led me to that place.

    EDGAR.   Bear free and patient thoughts. But who comes here? [*Enter* LEAR, *fantastically dressed with wild flowers*] The safer sense will ne'er accommodate his master thus.

LEAR.   No, they cannot touch me for coining; I am the king himself.

EDGAR.   O thou side-piercing sight!

LEAR.   Nature's above art in that respect. There's your press money. That fellow handles his bow like a crow-keeper: draw me a clothier's yard. Look, look! a mouse. Peace, peace! this piece of toasted cheese will do 't. There's my gauntlet; I'll prove it on a giant. Bring up the brown bills. O! well flown, bird; i' the clout, i' the clout: hewgh! Give the word.

EDGAR.   Sweet marjoram.

LEAR.   Pass.

GLOUCESTER.   I know that voice.

LEAR.   Ha! Goneril, with a white beard! They flattered me like a dog, and told me I had white hairs in my beard ere the black ones were there. To say "ay" and "no" to every thing I said! "Ay" and "no" too was no good divinity. When the rain came to wet me once and the wind to make me chatter, when the thunder would not peace at my bidding, there I found 'em, there I smelt 'em out. Go to, they are not men o' their words: they told me I was everything; 'tis a lie, I am not ague-proof.

GLOUCESTER.   The trick of that voice I do well remember: is 't not the king?

LEAR   Ay, every inch a king:
When I do stare, see how the subject quakes.
I pardon that man's life. What was thy cause?
Adultery?
Thou shalt not die: die for adultery! No:
The wren goes to 't, and the small gilded fly
Does lecher in my sight.
Let copulation thrive; for Gloucester's bastard son
Was kinder to his father than my daughters
Got 'tween the lawful sheets.
To 't, luxury, pell-mell! for I lack soldiers.
Behold yond simpering dame,
Whose face between her forks presageth snow;
That minces virtue, and does shake the head
To hear of pleasure's name;
The fitchew nor the soiled horse goes to 't
With a more riotous appetite.

Down from the waist they are Centaurs,
Though women all above:
But to the girdle do the gods inherit,
Beneath is all the fiend's:

There's hell, there's darkness, there's the sulfurous pit, burning, scalding, stench, consumption; fie, fie, fie! pah, pah! Give me an ounce of civet, good apothecary, to sweeten my imagination: there's money for thee.

GLOUCESTER.   O! Let me kiss that hand.

LEAR.   Let me wipe it first; it smells of mortality.

GLOUCESTER.   O ruin'd piece of nature! This great world shall so wear out to naught. Dost thou know me?

LEAR.   I remember thine eyes well enough. Dost thou squiny at me? No, do thy worst, blind Cupid; I'll not love. Read thou this challenge; mark but the penning of it.

GLOUCESTER.   Were all thy letters suns, I could not see.

EDGAR [aside].   I would not take this from report; it is, and my heart breaks at it.

LEAR.   Read.

GLOUCESTER.   What! with the case of eyes?

LEAR.   O, ho! are you there with me? No eyes in your head, nor no money in your purse? Your eyes are in a heavy case, your purse in a light: yet you see how this world goes.

GLOUCESTER.　I see it feelingly.

LEAR.　What! art mad? A man may see how this world goes with no eyes. Look with thine ears: see how yond justice rails upon yond simple thief. Hark, in thine ear: change places, and, handy-dandy, which is the justice, which is the thief? Thou hast seen a farmer's dog bark at a beggar?

GLOUCESTER.　Ay, sir.

LEAR.　And the creature run from the cur? There thou might'st behold the great image of authority; a dog's obeyed in office.

> Thou rascal beadle, hold thy bloody hand!
> Why dost thou lash that whore? Strip thine own back;
> Thou hotly lusts to use her in that kind
> For which thou whipp'st her. The usurer hangs the
>　　cozener.
> Through tatter'd clothes small vices do appear;
> Robes and furr'd gowns hide all. Plate sin with gold,
> And the strong lance of justice hurtless breaks;
> Arm it in rags, a pigmy's straw does pierce it.
> None does offend, none, I say, none; I'll able 'em:
> Take that of me, my friend, who have the power
> To seal the accuser's lips. Get thee glass eyes;
> And, like a scurvy politician, seem
> To see the things thou dost not. Now, now, now, now;
> Pull off my boots; harder, harder; so.

EDGAR [aside].　O! matter and impertinency mix'd; reason in madness.

LEAR.　If thou wilt weep my fortunes, take my eyes; I know thee well enough; thy name is Gloucester; thou must be patient; we came crying hither: thou know'st the first time that we smell the air we waul and cry. I will preach to thee: mark.

GLOUCESTER.　Alack, alack the day!

LEAR.　When we are born, we cry that we are come to this great stage of fools. This' a good block! It were a delicate stratagem to shoe a troop of horse with felt; I'll put 't in proof, and when I have stol'n upon these sons-in-law, then, kill, kill, kill, kill, kill, kill!

Enter a Gentleman, with Attendants.

GENTLEMAN.   O! here he is; lay hand upon him. Sir, your most
dear daughter—

LEAR.   No rescue? What! a prisoner? I am even the natural fool
of fortune. Use me well; you shall have ransom. Let me have
surgeons; I am cut to the brains.

GENTLEMAN.   You shall have anything.

LEAR.   No seconds? all myself? Why this would make a man a
man of salt, to use his eyes for garden waterpots, ay, and for laying
autumn's dust.

GENTLEMAN.   Good sir—

LEAR.   I will die bravely, like a bridegroom. What! I will be
jovial: come, come; I am a king, my masters, know you that?

GENTLEMAN.   You are a royal one, and we obey you.

LEAR.   Then there's life in 't. Nay, an you get it, you shall get it
by running. Sa, sa, sa, sa.   *Exit running. Attendants follow.*

GENTLEMAN
            A sight most pitiful in the meanest wretch,
            Past speaking of in a king! Thou hast one daughter,
            Who redeems nature from the general curse
            Which twain have brought her to.

EDGAR.   Hail, gentle sir!

GENTLEMAN.   Sir, speed you: what's your will?

EDGAR.   Do you hear aught, sir, of a battle toward?

GENTLEMAN.   Most sure and vulgar; every one hears that,
which can distinguish sound.

EDGAR.   But, by your favor, how near's the other army?

GENTLEMAN.   Near, and on speedy foot; the main descry stands
on the hourly thought.

EDGAR.   I thank you, sir: that's all.

GENTLEMAN.   Though that the queen on special cause is here,
her army is moved on.

EDGAR.   I thank you, sir.   *Exit Gentleman.*

GLOUCESTER.   You ever-gentle gods, take my breath from me:
let not my worser spirit tempt me again to die before you please!

EDGAR.   Well pray you, father.

GLOUCESTER.   Now, good sir, what are you?

EDGAR.   A most poor man, made tame to fortune's blows; who,

by the art of known and feeling sorrows, am pregnant to good pity.
Give me your hand, I'll lead you to some biding.

    GLOUCESTER.   Hearty thanks: the bounty and the benison of
heaven to boot, and boot!

Enter OSWALD.

    OSWALD.   A proclaim'd prize! Most happy! That eyeless head of
thine was first framed flesh to raise my fortunes. Thou old unhappy
traitor, briefly thyself remember: the sword is out that must destroy
thee.

    GLOUCESTER.   Now let thy friendly hand put strength enough
to 't.   EDGAR *interposes.*

    OSWALD.   Wherefore, bold peasant, darest thou support a

publish'd traitor? Hence; lest that the infection of his fortune take like hold on thee. Let go his arm.

EDGAR.   Chill not let go, zir, without vurther 'casion.

OSWALD.   Let go, slave, or thou diest.

EDGAR.   Good gentleman, go your gait, and let poor volk pass. An chud ha' bin zwaggered out of my life, 'twould not ha' bin zo long as 'tis by a vortnight. Nay, come not near th' old man; keep out, che vor ye, or Ise try whither your costard or my ballow be the harder. Chill be plain with you.

OSWALD.   Out, dunghill!

EDGAR.   Chill pick your teeth, zir. Come; no matter vor your foins.   *They fight, and* EDGAR *knocks him down.*

OSWALD.   Slave, thou hast slain me. Villain, take my purse. If ever thou wilt thrive, bury my body; and give the letters which thou find'st about me to Edmund Earl of Gloucester; seek him out upon the English party: O! untimely death. Death!

Dies.

EDGAR. I know thee well: a serviceable villain; as duteous to the vices of thy mistress as badness would desire.

GLOUCESTER. What! is he dead?

EDGAR. Sit you down, father; rest you. Let's see these pockets: the letters that he speaks of may be my friends. He's dead; I am only sorry he had no other deathsman. Let us see: leave, gentle wax; and, manners, blame us not: to know our enemies' minds, we'd rip their hearts; their papers is more lawful. *[Reads]* "Let our reciprocal vows be remembered. You have many opportunities to cut him off; if your will want not, time and place will be fruitfully offered. There is nothing done if he return the conqueror; then am I the prisoner, and his bed my jail; from the loathed warmth whereof deliver me, and supply the place for your labor.   Your—wife, so I would say—affectionate servant,   Goneril."

O undistinguish'd space of woman's will! A plot upon her virtuous husband's life, and the exchange my brother! Here, in the sands, thee I'll rake up, the post unsanctified of murderous lechers; and in the mature time with this ungracious paper strike the sight of the death-practiced duke. For him 'tis well that of thy death and business I can tell.

GLOUCESTER.   The king is mad: how stiff is my vile sense that I stand up, and have ingenious feeling of my huge sorrows! Better I were distract: so should my thoughts be sever'd from my griefs, and woes by wrong imaginations lose the knowledge of themselves.

A drum afar off.

EDGAR.   Give me your hand: far off, methinks, I hear the beaten drum. Come, father, I'll bestow you with a friend.

Exeunt.

SCENE VII.   *A Tent in the French Camp.*

Enter CORDELIA, KENT, *Doctor, and Gentleman.*

CORDELIA.   O thou good Kent! how shall I live and work to match thy goodness? My life will be too short, and every measure fail me.

KENT.   To be acknowledg'd, madam, is o'erpaid. All my reports go with the modest truth, nor more nor clipp'd, but so.

CORDELIA.   Be better suited: These weeds are memories of those worser hours: I prithee, put them off.

KENT.   Pardon, dear madam; yet to be known shortens my made intent: my boon I make it that you know me not till time and I think meet.

CORDELIA.   Then be 't so, my good lord. [*To the Doctor*] How does the king?

DOCTOR.   Madam, sleeps still.

CORDELIA.   O you kind gods, cure this great breach in his abused nature! The untuned and jarring senses, O! wind up of this child-changed father.

120

DOCTOR.   So please your majesty that we may wake the king?
he hath slept long.

CORDELIA.   Be govern'd by your knowledge, and proceed i' the
sway of your own will. Is he array'd?

Enter LEAR *in a chair carried by Servants.*

DOCTOR.   Ay, madam; in the heaviness of sleep we put fresh
garments on him.

KENT.   Be by, good madam, when we do awake him; I doubt
not of his temperance.

CORDELIA.   Very well.   *Music.*

DOCTOR.   Please you, draw near. Louder the music there!

CORDELIA.   O my dear father! Restoration hang thy medicine
on my lips, and let this kiss repair those violent harms that my two
sisters have in thy reverence made!

KENT.   Kind and dear princess!

CORDELIA.   Had you not been their father, these white flakes
          Had challenged pity of them. Was this a face
          To be opposed against the warring winds?

To stand against the deep dread-bolted thunder?
In the most terrible and nimble stroke
Of quick, cross lightning? to watch—poor perdu!
With this thin helm? Mine enemy's dog,
Though he had bit me, should have stood that night
Against my fire. And wast thou fain, poor father,
To hovel thee with swine and rogues forlorn,
In short and musty straw? Alack, alack!
'Tis wonder that thy life and wits at once
Had not concluded all. He wakes; speak to him.

DOCTOR.   Madam, do you; 'tis fittest.

CORDELIA.   How does my royal lord? How fares your majesty?

LEAR.   You do me wrong to take me out o' the grave; thou art a
soul in bliss; but I am bound upon a wheel of fire, that mine own
tears do scald like molten lead.

CORDELIA.   Sir, do you know me?

LEAR.   You are a spirit, I know; when did you die?

CORDELIA.   Still, still, far wide.

DOCTOR.   He's scarce awake; let him alone awhile.

LEAR.   Where have I been? Where am I? Fair daylight? I am
mightily abused. I should e'en die with pity to see another thus. I
know not what to say. I will not swear these are my hands: let's see; I
feel this pin prick. Would I were assured of my condition!

CORDELIA.   O! look upon me, sir, and hold your hands in
benediction o'er me. No, sir, you must not kneel.

LEAR.   Pray, do not mock me: I am a very foolish fond old man,
fourscore and upward, not an hour more nor less; and, to deal
plainly, I fear I am not in my perfect mind. Methinks I should know
you and know this man; yet I am doubtful: for I am mainly ignorant
what place this is, and all the skill I have remembers not these
garments; nor I know not where I did lodge last night. Do not laugh
at me; for, as I am a man, I think this lady to be my child Cordelia.

CORDELIA.   And so I am, I am.

LEAR.   Be your tears wet? Yes, faith. I pray, weep not: if you
have poison for me, I will drink it. I know you do not love me; for
your sisters have, as I do remember, done me wrong: you have some
cause, they have not.

CORDELIA.   No cause, no cause.

LEAR.   Am I in France?

KENT.   In your own kingdom, sir.

LEAR.   Do not abuse me.

DOCTOR.   Be comforted, good madam; the great rage, you see, is kill'd in him: and yet it is danger to make him even o'er the time he has lost. Desire him to go in; trouble him no more till further settling.

CORDELIA.   Will 't please your highness walk?

LEAR.   You must bear with me. Pray you now, forget and forgive: I am old and foolish.

     Exeunt LEAR, CORDELIA, *Doctor, and Attendants.*

GENTLEMAN.   Holds it true, sir, that the Duke of Cornwall was so slain?

KENT.   Most certain, sir.

GENTLEMAN.   Who is conductor of his people?

KENT.   As 'tis said, the bastard son of Gloucester.

GENTLEMAN.   They say Edgar, his banished son, is with the Earl of Kent in Germany.

KENT.   Report is changeable. 'Tis time to look about; the powers of the kingdom approach apace.

GENTLEMAN.   The arbitrement is like to be bloody. Fare you well, sir.   *Exit.*

KENT.   My point and period will be throughly wrought, or well or ill, as this day's battle's fought.   *Exit.*

ACT FIVE

SCENE I. *The British Camp near Dover.*

Enter, with drum and colors, EDMUND, REGAN, *Officers, Soldiers, and Others.*

EDMUND. Know of the duke if his last purpose hold, or whether since he is advis'd by aught to change the course; he's full of alteration and self-reproving; bring his constant pleasure.

To an Officer, who goes out.

REGAN. Our sister's man is certainly miscarried.

EDMUND. 'Tis to be doubted, madam.

REGAN. Now, sweet lord, you know the goodness I intend upon you: tell me, but truly, but then speak the truth, do you not love my sister?

EDMUND. In honor'd love.

REGAN. But have you never found my brother's way to the forfended place?

EDMUND. That thought abuses you.

REGAN. I am doubtful that you have been conjunct and bosom'd with her, as far as we call hers.

EDMUND. No, by mine honor, madam.

REGAN. I never shall endure her: dear my lord, be not familiar with her.

EDMUND. Fear me not. She and the duke her husband!

Enter, with drum and colors, ALBANY, GONERIL, *and Soldiers.*

GONERIL *[aside].* I had rather lose the battle than that sister should loosen him and me.

ALBANY. Our very loving sister, well bemet.
    Sir, this I heard; the king is come to his daughter,
    With others whom the rigor of our state
    Forced to cry out. Where I could not be honest,
    I never yet was valiant: for this business,
    It toucheth us, as France invades our land,
    Not bolds the king, with others, whom, I fear,
    Most just and heavy causes make oppose.

EDMUND. Sir, you speak nobly.

REGAN. Why is this reason'd?

GONERIL. Combine together 'gainst the enemy; for these domestic and particular broils art not the question here.

ALBANY.   Let's then determine with the ancient of war on our proceeding.

EDMUND.   I shall attend you presently at your tent.

REGAN.   Sister, you'll go with us?

GONERIL.   No.

REGAN.   'Tis most convenient; pray you, go with us.

GONERIL *[aside]*.   O, ho! I know the riddle. I will go.

As they are going out enter EDGAR, *disguised.*

EDGAR.   If e'er your grace had speech with man so poor, hear me one word.

ALBANY.   I'll overtake you. Speak.

Exeunt EDMUND, REGAN, GONERIL, *Officers, Soldiers, and Attendants.*

EDGAR.   Before you fight the battle, ope this letter. If you have victory, let the trumpet sound for him that brought it: wretched though I seem, I can produce a champion that will prove what is avouched there. If you miscarry, your business of the world hath so an end, and machination ceases. Fortune love you!

ALBANY.   Stay till I have read the letter.

EDGAR. I was forbid it. When time shall serve, let but the
herald cry, and I'll appear again.

ALBANY. Why, fare thee well: I will o'erlook thy paper.

Exit EDGAR.

Re-enter EDMUND.

EDMUND. The enemy's in view; draw up your powers. Here is
the guess of their true strength and forces by diligent discovery; but
your haste is now urged on you.

ALBANY. We will greet the time.   *Exit.*

EDMUND. To both these sisters have I sworn my love;
        Each jealous of the other, as the stung
        Are of the adder. Which of them shall I take?
        Both? one? or neither? Neither can be enjoy'd
        If both remain alive: to take the widow
        Exasperates, makes mad her sister Goneril;

And hardly shall I carry out my side,
Her husband being alive. Now then, we'll use
His countenance for the battle; which being done,
Let her who would be rid of him devise
His speedy taking off. As for the mercy
Which he intends to Lear and to Cordelia,
The battle done, and they within our power,
Shall never see his pardon; for my state
Stands on me to defend, not to debate.   *Exit.*

SCENE II.　　　　　　　　*A Field between the two Camps.*

Alarum within. Enter, with drum and colors, LEAR, CORDELIA, *and their Forces; and exeunt.*

　　　　　　　　　　　　　　　　　Enter EDGAR *and* GLOUCESTER.

EDGAR.　Here, father, take the shadow of this tree for your good host; pray that the right may thrive. If ever I return to you again, I'll bring you comfort.

GLOUCESTER.　Grace go with you, sir!　　　　　*Exit* EDGAR.

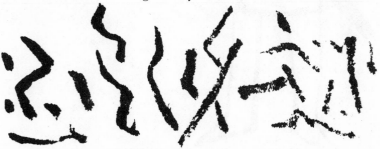

　　　　　Alarum; afterwards a retreat. Re-enter EDGAR.

EDGAR.　Away, old man! give me thy hand: away! King Lear hath lost, he and his daughter ta'en. Give me thy hand; come on.

GLOUCESTER.　No further, sir; a man may rot even here.

EDGAR.　What! in ill thoughts again? Men must endure their going hence, even as their coming hither: ripeness is all. Come on.

GLOUCESTER.　And that's true too.　　　　　*Exeunt.*

SCENE III.   *The British Camp near Dover.*

Enter, in conquest, with drum and colors, EDMUND, LEAR *and* CORDELIA, *prisoners; Officers, Soldiers, etc.*

EDMUND.   Some officers take them away: good guard, until their greater pleasures first be known that are to censure them.

CORDELIA. We are not the first who, with best meaning, have incurr'd the worst. For thee, oppressed king, am I cast down; myself could else out-frown false fortune's frown. Shall we not see these daughters and these sisters?

LEAR. No, no, no, no! Come, let's away to prison;
We two alone will sing like birds i' the cage:
When thou dost ask me blessing, I'll kneel down,
And ask of thee forgiveness: so we'll live,
And pray, and sing, and tell old tales, and laugh
At gilded butterflies, and hear poor rogues
Talk of court news; and we'll talk with them too,
Who loses and who wins; who's in, who's out;
And take upon 's the mystery of things,
As if we were God's spies: and we'll wear out,
In a wall'd prison, packs and sects of great ones
That ebb and flow by the moon.

EDMUND. Take them away.

LEAR. Upon such sacrifices, my Cordelia,
The gods themselves throw incense. Have I caught thee?
He that parts us shall bring a brand from heaven,
And fire us hence like foxes. Wipe thine eyes;
The goodyears shall devour them, flesh and fell,
Ere they shall make us weep: we'll see em starve first.
Come.   *Exeunt* LEAR *and* CORDELIA, *guarded.*

EDMUND. Come hither, captain; hark. Take thou this note; *[giving a paper]* Go follow them to prison. One step I have advanc'd thee; if thou dost as this instructs thee, thou dost make thy way to noble fortunes; know thou this, that men are as the time is; to be tender-minded does not become a sword; thy great employment will not bear question; either say thou 'lt do 't, or thrive by other means.

OFFICER.   I'll do 't, my lord.

EDMUND.   About it; and write happy when thou hast done. Mark—I say, instantly, and carry it so as I have set it down.

OFFICER.   I cannot draw a cart nor eat dried oats; if it be man's work I'll do it.   *Exit.*

Flourish. Enter ALBANY, GONERIL, REGAN, *Officers, and Attendants.*

ALBANY.   Sir, you have show'd today your valiant strain, and fortune led you well; you have the captives who were the opposites of this day's strife; we do require them of you, so to use them as we shall find their merits and our safety may equally determine.

EDMUND.   Sir, I thought it fit to send the old and miserable king to some retention and appointed guard; whose age has charms in it, whose title more, to pluck the common bosom on his side, and turn our impress'd lances in our eyes which do command them. With him I sent the queen; my reason all the same; and they are ready tomorrow, or at further space, to appear where you shall hold your session. At this time we sweat and bleed; the friend hath lost his friend, and the best quarrels, in the heat, are cursed by those that feel their sharpness; the question of Cordelia and her father requires a fitter place.

ALBANY.   Sir, by your patience, I hold you but a subject of this war, not as a brother.

REGAN.   That's as we list to grace him: methinks our pleasure might have been demanded, ere you had spoke so far. He led our powers, bore the commission of my place and person; the which immediacy may well stand up, can call itself your brother.

GONERIL.   Not so hot; in his own grace he doth exalt himself more than in your addition.

REGAN.   In my rights, by me invested, he compeers the best.

ALBANY.   That were the most, if he should husband you.

REGAN.   Jesters do oft prove prophets.

GONERIL.   Holla, holla! That eye that told you so look'd but a-squint.

REGAN.   Lady, I am not well; else I should answer from a full-flowing stomach. General, take thou my soldiers, prisoners, patrimony; dispose of them, of me; the walls are thine; witness the world, that I create thee here my lord and master.

GONREIL.   Mean you to enjoy him?

ALBANY.   The let-alone lies not in your good will.

EDMUND.   Nor in thine, lord.

ALBANY.   Half-blooded fellow, yes.

REGAN [*to* EDMUND].   Let the drum strike, and prove my title thine.

ALBANY.   Stay yet; hear reason. Edmund, I arrest thee
    On capital treason; and, in thy arrest,
    This gilded serpent.   *Pointing to* GONERIL.
    For your claim, fair sister,
    I bar it in the interest of my wife;
    'Tis she is subcontracted to this lord,
    And I, her husband, contradict your bans.
    If you will marry, make your loves to me,
    My lady is bespoke.

GONERIL.   An interlude!

ALBANY.   Thou art arm'd, Gloucester; let the trumpet sound:
    If none appear to prove upon thy person
    Thy heinous, manifest, and many teasons,
    There is my pledge;   *Throws down a glove.*

I'll make it on thy heart,
Ere I taste bread, thou art in nothing less
Than I have here proclaim'd thee.

REGAN.   Sick! O, sick!

GONERIL *[aside]*.   If not, I'll ne'er trust medicine.

EDMUND.   There's my exchange: *Throws down a glove.*
What in the world he is
That names me traitor, villain-like he lies.
Call by thy trumpet: he that dares approach,
On him, on you, who not? I will maintain
My truth and honor firmly.

ALBANY.   A herald, ho!

EDMUND.   A herald, ho! A herald!

ALBANY.   Trust to thy single virtue; for thy soldiers, all levied in
my name, have in my name took their discharge.

REGAN.   My sickness grows upon me.

ALBANY.   She is not well; convey her to my tent.

Exit REGAN, *led.*

Enter a Herald.

Come hither, herald—let the trumpet sound—and read out this.

OFFICER. Sound, trumpet! *[A trumpet sounds.]*

HERALD *[reads].* "If any man of quality or degree within the lists of the army will maintain upon Edmund, supposed Earl of Gloucester, that he is a manifold traitor, let him appear by the third sound of the trumpet. He is bold in his defense."

EDMUND.   Sound!

[First trumpet.]
HERALD.   Again!
[Second trumpet.]
HERALD.   Again!
[Third trumpet.]
[Trumpet answers within.]
[Enter EDGAR, *armed, with a trumpet before him.]*

ALBANY.   Ask him his purposes, why he appears upon this call o' the trumpet.

HERALD.   What are you? your name? your quality? and why you answer this present summons?

EDGAR.   Know, my name is lost; by treason's tooth bare-gnawn, and canker-bit: yet am I noble as the adversary I come to cope.

ALBANY.   Which is that adversary?

EDGAR.   What's he that speaks for Edmund Earl of Gloucester?

EDMUND.   Himself: what say'st thou to him?

EDGAR.   Draw thy sword,
That, if my speech offend a noble heart,
Thy arm may do thee justice; here is mine:
Behold, it is the privilege of mine honors,
My oath, and my profession: I protest,
Maugre thy strength, youth, place, and eminence,
Despite thy victor sword and fire-new fortune,
Thy valor and thy heart, thou art a traitor,
False to thy gods, thy brother, and thy father,
Conspirant 'gainst this high illustrious prince,
And, from the extremest upward of thy head
To the descent and dust below thy foot,

A most toad-spotted traitor. Say thou "No,"
This sword, this arm, and my best spirits are bent
To prove upon thy heart, whereto I speak,
Thou liest.

EDMUND. In wisdom I should ask thy name;
But since thy outside looks so fair and warlike,
And that thy tongue some say of breeding breathes,
What safe and nicely I might well delay
By rule of knighthood, I disdain and spurn;
Back do I toss these treasons to thy head,
With the hell-hated lie o'erwhelm thy heart,
Which, for they yet glance by and scarcely bruise,
This sword of mine shall give them instant way,
Where they shall rest for ever. Trumpets, speak.

Alarums. They fight. EDMUND *falls.*

ALBANY. Save him! save him!

GONERIL. This is practice, Gloucester: by the law of arms thou wast not bound to answer an unknown opposite; thou art not vanquish'd, but cozen'd and beguil'd.

ALBANY.   Shut your mouth, dame, or with this paper shall I stop it. Hold, sir; thou worse than any name, read thine own evil: no tearing, lady; I perceive you know it.   *Gives the letter to* EDMUND.

GONERIL.   Say, if I do, the laws are mine, not thine: who can arraign me for 't.   *Exit.*

ALBANY.   Most monstrous! O! Know'st thou this paper?

EDMUND.   Ask me not what I know.

ALBANY.   Go after her: she's desperate; govern her.

Exit an Officer.

EDMUND.   What you have charged me with, that have I done,
And more, much more; the time will bring it out:
'Tis past, and so am I. But what art thou
That has this fortune on me? If thou'rt noble,
I do forgive thee.

EDGAR.   Let's exchange charity.
I am no less in blood than thou art, Edmund;
If more, the more thou hast wrong'd me.
My name is Edgar, and thy father's son.
The gods are just, and of our pleasant vices
Make instruments to plague us:
The dark and vicious place where thee he got
Cost him his eyes.

EDMUND.   Thou has spoken right, 'tis true. The wheel is come full circle; I am here.

ALBANY.   Methought thy very gait did prophesy a royal noble-ness: I must embrace thee: let sorrow split my heart, if ever I did hate thee or thy father.

EDGAR.   Worthy prince, I know 't.

ALBANY.   Where have you hid yourself? How have you known the miseries of your father?

EDGAR.   By nursing them, my lord. List a brief tale; and when 'tis told, O! that my heart would burst, the bloody proclamation to escape that follow'd me so near—O! our lives' sweetness, that we the pain of death would hourly die rather than die at once!—taught me to shift into a madman's rags, to assume a semblance that very dogs disdain'd: and in this habit met I my father with his bleeding rings, their precious stones new lost; became his guide, led him, begg'd for him, sav'd him from despair; never—O fault! reveal'd myself unto him, until some half-hour past, when I was arm'd; not sure, though

hoping, of this good success, I ask'd his blessing, and from first to last told him my pilgrimage: but his flaw'd heart—alack! too weak the conflict to support!—'twixt two extremes of passion, joy and grief, burst smilingly.

EDMUND. This speech of yours hath moved me, and shall

perchance do good; but speak you on; you look as you had something
more to say.

ALBANY. If there be more, more woeful, hold it in; for I am
almost ready to dissolve, hearing of this.

EDGAR. This would have seem'd a period
To such as love not sorrow; but another,
To amplify too much, would make much more,
And top extremity.
Whilst I was big in clamor came there a man,
Who, having seen me in my worst estate,
Shunn'd my abhorr'd society; but then, finding
Who 't was that so endured, with his strong arms

He fasten'd on my neck, and bellow'd out
As he'd burst heaven; threw him on my father;
Told the most piteous tale of Lear and him
That ever ear received; which in recounting
His grief grew puissant, and the strings of life
Began to crack: twice then the trumpets sounded,
And there I left him tranced.

ALBANY. But who was this?

EDGAR. Kent, sir, the banish'd Kent; who in disguise
Follow'd his enemy king, and did him service
Improper for a slave.

Enter a Gentleman, with a bloody knife.

GENTLEMAN. Help, help! O, help!

EDGAR. What kind of help?

ALBANY. Speak, man.

EDGAR. What means that bloody knife?

GENTLEMAN. 'Tis hot, it smokes; it came even from the heart of—O! she's dead.

ALBANY. Who dead? speak, man.

GENTLEMAN. Your lady, sir, your lady: and her sister by her is poisoned; she confesses it.

EDMUND. I was contracted to them both: all three now marry in an instant.

EDGAR. Here comes Kent.

ALBANY. Produce the bodies, be they alive or dead: *[Exit Gentleman]* this judgment of the heavens, that makes us tremble, touches us not with pity. *[Enter KENT]* O! is this he? The time will not allow the compliment which very manners urges.

KENT. I am come to bid my king and master aye good night; is he not here?

ALBANY. Great thing of us forgot! Speak, Edmund, where's the king? and where's Cordelia? Seest thou this object, Kent?

The bodies of GONERIL *and* REGAN *are brought in.*

KENT. Alack! why thus?

EDMUND. Yet Edmund was belov'd: the one the other poison'd for my sake, and after slew herself.

ALBANY. Even so. Cover their faces.

EDMUND.   I pant for life: some good I mean to do
           Despite of mine own nature. Quickly send,
           Be brief in it, to the castle; for my writ
           Is on the life of Lear and on Cordelia.
           Nay, send in time.
ALBANY.   Run, run! O, run!
EDGAR.   To who, my lord? Who has the office? send thy token
of reprieve.
EDMUND.   Well thought on: take my sword, give it the captain.
ALBANY.   Haste thee, for thy life.   *Exit* EDGAR.
EDMUND.   He hath commission from thy wife and me to hang
Cordelia in the prison, and to lay the blame upon her own despair,
that she fordid herself.
ALBANY.   The gods defend her! Bear him hence awhile.

                                                   EDMUND *is borne off.*

Re-enter LEAR, *with* CORDELIA *dead in his arms;* EDGAR, *Officer,
and Others.*

LEAR.   Howl, howl, howl, howl! O! you are men of stones:
           Had I your tongues and eyes, I'd use them so
           That heaven's vault should crack. She's gone for ever.
           I know when one is dead, and when one lives;
           She's dead as earth. Lend me a looking glass;
           If that her breath will mist or stain the stone,
           Why, then she lives.
KENT.   Is this the promis'd end?
EDGAR.   Or image of that horror?
ALBANY.   Fall and cease.
LEAR.   This feather stirs; she lives! if it be so, it is a chance
which does redeem all sorrows that ever I have felt.
KENT *[kneeling].*   O my good master!
LEAR.   Prithee, away.
EDGAR.   'Tis noble Kent, your friend.
LEAR.   A plague upon you, murderous traitors all!
           I might have sav'd her; now, she's gone for ever!
           Cordelia, Cordelia! stay a little. Ha!
           What is 't thou say'st? Her voice was ever soft,
           Gentle and low, an excellent thing in woman.
           I kill'd the slave that was a-hanging thee.

OFFICER. 'Tis true, my lords, he did.

LEAR. Did I not, fellow? I have seen the day, with my good biting falchion I would have made them skip: I am old now, and these same crosses spoil me. Who are you? Mine eyes are not o' the best: I'll tell you straight.

KENT. If fortune brag of two she lov'd and hated, one of them we behold.

LEAR. This' a dull sight. Are you not Kent?

KENT. The same; your servant Kent. Where is your servant Caius?

LEAR. He's a good fellow, I can tell you that; he'll strike, and quickly too. He's dead and rotten.

KENT. No, my good lord; I am the very man—

LEAR. I'll see that straight.

KENT. That from your first of difference and decay, have follow'd your sad steps—

LEAR. You are welcome hither.

KENT.   Nor no man else. All's cheerless, dark, and deadly: your eldest daughters have fordone themselves, and desperately are dead.

LEAR.   Ay, so I think.

ALBANY.   He knows not what he says, and vain is it that we present us to him.

EDGAR.   Very bootless.

Enter an Officer.

OFFICER.   Edmund is dead, my lord.

ALBANY.   That's but a trifle here. You lords and noble friends, know our intent; what comfort to this great decay may come shall be applied: for us, we will resign, during the life of this old majesty, to him our absolute power: [*To* EDGAR *and* KENT] You, to your rights, with boot and such addition as your honors have more than merited. All friends shall taste the wages of their virtue, and all foes the cup of their deservings. O! see, see!

LEAR.   And my poor fool is hang'd! No, no, no life!
             Why should a dog, a horse, a rat, have life,
             And thou no breath at all? Thou 'lt come no more,
             Never, never, never, never, never!
             Pray you, undo this button: thank you, sir.
             Do you see this? Look on her, look, her lips,
             Look there, look there!   *Dies.*

EDGAR.   He faints! My lord, my lord!

KENT.   Break, heart; I prithee, break!

EDGAR.   Look up, my lord.

KENT.   Vex not his ghost: O! let him pass; he hates him
That would upon the rack of this tough world
Stretch him out longer.

EDGAR.   He is gone, indeed.

KENT.   The wonder is he hath endur'd so long: he but usurp'd
his life.

ALBANY.　Bear them from hence. Our present business is general woe. [*To* KENT *and* EDGAR] Friends of my soul, you twain rule in this realm, and the gor'd state sustain.

KENT.　　I have a journey, sir, shortly to go; my master calls me, I must not say no.

EDGAR.　　The weight of this sad time we must obey;
Speak what we feel, not what we ought to say.
The oldest hath borne most: we that are young
Shall never see so much, nor live so long.

Exeunt, with a dead march.

Afterword

Although written nearly four hundred years ago, *King Lear* continues to provoke the interest, curiosity, and admiration of twentieth-century scholars, critics, and just plain readers or playgoers. Like other cherished works of art, great poems, paintings, sculpture, novels, and music, the play has been subjected to an almost unbelievable amount of attentive, and frequently intelligent, scrutiny. The root cause, I believe, of this attention is that the play has power. It tells us something important about ourselves, and therefore it is loved. And like most things that we love, it is transmitted, preserved, and interpreted for each succeeding generation. Those who come to know *King Lear* recognize that it enhances life, that it reveals or clarifies some of the basic conditions of our humanity. And by revealing and clarifying, the play liberates us and is therefore supremely significant, priceless, worthy of sustained and careful contemplation. Subjected to such concentrated analysis, the play poses all kinds of difficulties and questions. Thus it is that scholars and critics, men and women who have devoted their lives to the study of literature, take upon themselves the task of providing answers to whatever problems arise from a contemplation of the text—from questions about punctuation, spelling, or lineation to speculations on the relationship of *King Lear* to political theory, Christian doctrine, or psychoanalysis.

151

The first question scholars ask is, what is the true text of *King Lear*? Do we have the play in the form that Shakespeare intended? This question is not easy to answer, for the play comes to us in two versions, neither of which, as far as we know, was approved by the author. *King Lear* was first published in 1608 in a quarto volume, and reproduced in 1619. The second version appeared in 1623, in the so-called First Folio edition of Shakespeare's collected plays. The versions are markedly different. The Folio version omits three hundred lines of the Quarto, while adding one hundred new lines. Furthermore, there are many verbal alterations in the Folio text. To make matters worse, none of the twelve existing copies of the Quarto version are exactly alike. In short, while we know what Shakespeare intended in general and large part, we are not sure of certain details, of the dozens of "variants" between the Quarto and Folio texts.

Establishing the validity of these variants has been the laborious and tricky task of the scholarly editors of *King Lear*. The most respected modern editors, G. I. Duthie, Kenneth Muir, and Alfred Harbage (whose excellent editions have been consulted in preparation of the Beacon text), generally accept the authority of the Folio version but add lines or substitute words from the Quarto where such addition or substitution seems dramatically sensible and historically accurate. These editors also print alternate variants either in footnotes or in an appendix so that a fellow scholar or student might check and ponder a rejected reading. By means of their meticulous care and useful erudition, these scholars do us a great service. They provide a text of the play that is generally accepted and authoritative (although uncertainties remain and are argued in the pages of learned journals).

Once the text is established, other questions need answers. Where did the story come from? What did Shakespeare use as a source for *King Lear*? The editors mentioned above, and others, have investigated this problem and concluded that Shakespeare drew on several contemporary sources—among the most obvious, an old chronicle play, *The True Chronicle History of King Leir*, published in 1605 but probably known to Shakespeare before that date; the historian Holinshed's account of King Lear in his *Chronicles*; Edmund Spenser's brief account of the King in *The Faerie Queene*; and what appears to be the basis of the Gloucester sub-plot as it occurs in Sir Philip Sidney's *Arcadia*.

Using evidence internal and external to *King Lear*, scholars have ascertained that the play was written between 1603 and Christmas 1606 (when we know it was performed), probably in the winter of 1604–1605. To date its composition more precisely seems impossible, at present, although scholars are constantly searching for new and more accurate evidence. In the main, however, the larger textual and bibliographical questions about *King Lear* have been answered by the literary historians working in the past two centuries.

Questions arising from the lines and words of the text itself are also answered by textual editors. Sometimes the very meaning or dramatic relationship of a speech or word may not be perfectly clear. Editors then provide the reader with a scholarly interpretation or lexical definition based on dramatic or contemporary evidence in an effort to state as accurately as possible the precise connotation of each word. Difficult speeches, odd locutions, and tangled syntax are often paraphrased in a footnote by an editor in words that he thinks express the meaning of the lines. Almost all of Shakespeare's plays and almost all of our older literature contain these textual, lexical, and grammatical difficulties, and *King Lear* not the least.

Yet most of the problems of language one encounters in reading *King Lear* are soluble if the reader attends carefully to the context in which the difficulty occurs. Then definitions and clarification, while not totally precise, will arise from the way a word is used, how it is placed with, and refers to, other words, and what in general the speaker is saying. When Lear uses the word "meads" in the description of his kingdom, we can easily see that the word probably means *meadows*. The context similarly defines "trice" as *quick* or *quickly*, "buzz" as a slang term for *rumor*, and "kite" as a ravenous animal of some kind, probably a bird. (What we may not know is that a kite is a kind of hawk, a predator and eater of carrion, which hovers above its prey. Hence the toy is named after the bird.) We may not know the precise meanings of all the names Kent calls the steward Oswald, but from the context we can guess that "clotpoll" is not a compliment and means *dunce* or *numskull*. We need to be told, however, that in calling Oswald a "whoreson zed," Kent is likening him to the letter Z, regarded as an "unnecessary letter" because it was not in the Latin alphabet and thus ignored in contemporary dictionaries.

Some words in the play are archaic but still current in

specialized ways. Thus "messes" meaning *portions of food* is still found in the military mess hall. The word "weeds" for clothes may be heard in references to the black clothes worn by widows. "Germens" meaning *seeds* is found in "germinate" or "wheat germ." Terms still current in legal jargon appear in the play: "capable" meaning *able to inherit* and "attaint" meaning *impeachment*.

Most of the difficult words in *King Lear* are a result of the language's being nearly four hundred years old, yet we are agreeably surprised to find Shakespeare's vocabulary to be largely our own, except in a few instances. Some words are puzzling because they describe a thing that is archaic, an object we no longer see in daily life. Thus when the Fool talks of a codpiece, he is referring to an item of Elizabethan male clothing, a garment that covered the crotch and genitals. Once we know this fact, we can see that he uses "codpiece" as a metaphor for the phallus and thus as a basis of one of his many sexual jokes. Some of us may have seen an animal jump suddenly when spurred or goaded, and this may help us to understand the phrase "on the gad," i.e., on the goad, as *suddenly*. Although we no longer have licensed fools, we know that fools traditionally wore a cap called a coxcomb.

Sometimes the language seems perfectly clear, when in fact, after some study and knowledge, the meaning shifts. When Kent calls Oswald a "base football player," we think we know what he means, but the insult is sharpened when we discover that in Shakespeare's time noisy and disreputable urchins played a game something like modern soccer in the streets of London, much to the annoyance of older and more respected citizens. In the same way we might misunderstand Edgar when, in referring to his "closet," he means his room and not a place to hang clothes.

Then there are the words, not very many, whose use and meaning have simply dropped out of modern English. These must be bluntly defined. Edmund's "moiety" is his *share*. "Trowest," spoken by the Fool, is a form of the verb *trow*, to believe. "Kibes" are either chilblains or chapped heels. A "sumpter" is a *pack horse*. "Snuffs and packings" is a slang phrase for *quarrels and plots*; whereas "festinate" and "oeilliads" are high-falutin words for *hasty* and *amorous glances*.

These last examples testify to the astonishing range of Shakespeare's vocabulary and the freedom with which he could use either bookish or slang words. He was thus capable of brilliant and daring images. Toward the end of the play Cordelia describes the suffering Lear as "poor *perdu*." With a single word the king's state is superbly characterized, for *perdu* carries its French meaning, a "lost one," and its military connotation, "an isolated, endangered sentry." In his madness and separation from sympathetic companions Lear is both lost and dangerously isolated.

The most difficult task for editors of *King Lear* is to make sense of the riddling speeches of the Fool, the ravings—feigned or genuine—of Tom o' Bedlam and Lear, and the numerous allusions to gods, goddesses, places, and literary sources. The allusions may be explained in most good encyclopedias, while a careful reading of the wild talk of the Fool, Lear, and Tom o' Bedlam will often provide adequate illumination. Consulting a scholarly edition of the text will provide even more. Yet even after such effort, we might well agree that *King Lear* contains some puzzling though splendid passages, best described as ". . . matter and impertinency mixed; / Reason in madness."

Once the validity of the text is established and the meanings of the words are made as clear as possible, the larger and perhaps more interesting questions of interpretation arise. It is here that the reader may silently join the great conversation about *King Lear* that has been in progress for more than three hundred years. Such various and distinguished literary thinkers as Dr. Samuel Johnson, John Keats, Samuel Taylor Coleridge, A. C. Bradley, and Leo Tolstoy have written about the play, tried to clarify its shifting intricacy or to articulate its ultimate meaning. None has succeeded completely, for as times change, attitudes to the play also change. Yet it is surprising how often modern critics go back to Johnson or Coleridge and find in their comments (if not their judgments) the essential and eternal problems with which *King Lear* challenges the reader.

In the twentieth century, literally hundreds—perhaps thousands—of books, articles, and parts of books have been written about *King Lear*. Each has something of interest, although some critical interpretations are, of course, better than others—fresher, more comprehensive (and comprehensible), or more illuminating for the contemporary reader. At any rate the sheer mass of modern commentary on *King Lear* is formidable. As a result, a reader interested in discovering more about the play is put off when confronted by the immense bibliography *King Lear* has generated. Where does he begin?

The following paragraphs are meant to engage the interested reader in the continuing discussion of *King Lear* by introducing him to eight fairly recent studies of the play. The introductory nature of the largely descriptive comments below should be emphasized, for they do not pretend to do justice to the subtle complexity and sensitive and scholarly analyses these books contain. Moreover, it should be said that these are not necessarily the best books written on the play. They happen to be the ones that have given me pleasure *and* illumination. It therefore is hoped that the reader who is intrigued by the play will find any one of these books valuable as a guide to a deeper, richer understanding of Shakespeare's great and enduring drama.

Almost all the critics—including those mentioned here—see *King Lear* in terms of dualities, either as a dramatized conflict of two Natures (Nature as lawless and indifferent and Nature as ordered and beneficent), or as ironic oppositions of appearance and reality, reason and emotion, knowledge and wisdom, faith and doubt, individual man and society, and so on. Although it is a truism that every drama expresses some conflict, *King Lear* is unusual in that it seems to be *all* conflict, a network of oppositions of varying intensity, each related to the other. No one conflict seems to control entirely the development of the action. Having these dualities, the play thus generates situations of irony and paradox, unexpected reversal, confusions of identity, and riddling illusion.

While all critics have recognized the overwhelming and pervasive ironies in the play, they differ as to how these conflicts should be understood. Some say the play is unresolved; others offer interpretations providing either a total or a partial resolution. There is space to mention only one example of the play's several ironies, yet it is perhaps the central and most disturbing of all. Most critics, and readers, too, are uneasy about the conclusion of *King Lear*, especially the almost freakish and senseless death of Cordelia. The end may be tragically and dramatically powerful, but it seems radically unjust and unsatisfying. What does the ending *mean?* That question exercises the interpreting critic who writes both to possess and share his conception of the drama.

Two critics writing in the 1940s see the play as resolved

ultimately on the basis of Christian principles. Robert B. Heilman, in his book *This Great Stage: Image and Structure in King Lear*, reaches his conclusion by a meticulous examination of recurrent words and patterns of poetic and dramatic elements that build up themes of blindness, order in nature, nakedness, and madness. Having isolated these themes, each of which contributes to the "total metaphor" of the play, Heilman carefully analyzes such ironic dualities as appearance and reality, the Nature of Man and the Nature of Nature, madness and reason, and man and the gods. The principles of religious faith—notably as they are expressed in the character of Cordelia—reconcile these opposites, relate the thematic patterns to one another, and, according to Heilman, thereby account for the universal appeal of *King Lear*.

In *Shakespeare's Doctrine of Nature, A Study of King Lear*, John F. Danby begins with an excellent discussion of conflicting concepts of Nature in Shakespeare's time, a conflict which, in turn, created a divided idea of Reason, regarded either as a moral guide or as an instrumental means. This division leads to a notion of two societies based on differing ethical systems. The characters in the play are thus placed in a field of choice. Edmund, as the prime example of one who regards Nature as Hobbesian warfare and Reason merely as a practical tool to achieve personal ends, is analyzed in detail. The genesis of his character, the "machiavel," is traced through Shakespeare's earlier plays. Danby is especially illuminating in his discussion of the speeches of the Fool, whose riddles and songs seesaw between the opposed dualities. Arguing that the major characters carry symbolic and perhaps allegorical significance, Danby provides some compelling analyses of the characters of Cordelia, who represents unifying and unified Nature, and Lear, who in his symbolic role as king stands potentially for all men. Lear's corruption and decline are therefore crimes against all men and also violations of ordered Nature. His recovery illustrates a process of regeneration based on the Christian principles of charity, reconciliation, and redemption in a fallen world. Finally, the play, having as its main thematic conflict the problems of a "good man in a bad society," criticizes and then resolves the larger political questions that motivate the dramatic action.

Two very scholarly books place *King Lear* in its contemporary setting. Russell A. Fraser, in *Shakespeare's Poetics in Relation to*

King Lear, shows how Shakespeare exploited the conventional images and thoughts of his time. Using verbal and pictorial evidence, Fraser demonstrates that the major themes in *King Lear* had great currency in Elizabethan and Jacobean times. Providence, Kind (relationships), Fortune, Anarchy and Order, Reason and Will, Show and Substance, and Redemption were vigorously discussed and argued by Shakespeare's contemporaries. With impressive erudition, Fraser then shows how these predominantly dualistic abstractions run through all of the plays, and particularly how they generate conflict in *King Lear*.

Like Fraser, William R. Elton, in *King Lear and the Gods*, reconstructs the intellectual setting in which *King Lear* first appeared. He pays particular attention to Renaissance debates about Providence, the development of skepticism and empiricism, Calvinist ideas of predestination and man's fallen state and the consequent limits placed on man's powers of reason and comprehension, and, finally, the surprisingly widespread atheism of the period. Each of these topics, illustrated with masses of quotations from Elizabethan authors, is related to the action of the play.

Arguing that *King Lear* is a pagan, non-Christian drama, Elton demonstrates this premise by comparing Shakespeare's play and the earlier and obviously Christian drama of *King Leir* (ca. 1588–1594). This comparison leads to a discussion of the major non-Christian themes Elton sees in *King Lear*.

Cordelia and Edgar enact the idea of "Prisca Theologia," that is, that pagans (those without a knowledge of Christian doctrine) can, by means of virtue and fidelity to the bonds of humanity, achieve a kind of grace. Goneril, Regan, and Edmund are examples of "Pagan Atheism," of those who believe only in pragmatic force, quantity not quality, and who are motivated by lawless and egocentric greed. Gloucester, helpless before irrational magic, believing himself to be controlled by unknown and unknowable forces, is an example of "Pagan Superstition."

King Lear's relationship to the gods shifts in the course of the play. Beginning as a pious though complacent believer in Nature, he gradually loses his faith in divine powers. Through suffering and degradation he comes to see that the heavens are ambiguous, indifferent to justice or injustice. The gods may not be there at all; hence the principle he enacts is that of the "Deus Absconditus," the god who is irrevocably hidden or concealed.

Elton ends his learned, thoughtful, and comprehensive study by concluding that *King Lear*, informed by explicit and structural irony, lacking an ordered pattern, without poetic or any other kind of justice, reveals man's condition to be only that of suffering and illusion. Thus it is not at all an optimistic Christian play; it leaves us with a confusion of values, yet stands as Shakespeare's profound and troubling attempt to illustrate the irreconcilable ethical, moral, and religious conflicts of his time and our own.

Marvin Rosenberg's *The Masks of King Lear* is valuable in several respects. In addition to providing the reader with a sound critical interpretation of the play, interesting discussions of the main characters, and a scene-by-scene analysis of the whole, Rosenberg firmly and consistently relates *King Lear* to its stage history. His analyses thus contain comments and interpretations by distinguished directors, actors, and producers as well as remarks based on his own wide-ranging research and personal experience of numerous staged and filmed performances. In reading Rosenberg we are given a history of the play's stage life as well as a useful understanding of how actors and directors have regarded *King Lear* and the dramaturgical problems—both practical and interpretive—it presents. The sources of the hundreds of interesting comments Rosenberg quotes (frequently from tapes of interviews with well-known actors) are detailed in a full and useful bibliography.

Two critics place *King Lear* in its historical context in an effort to reach interpretations that conform with the play but have validity in the present. The title of Paul A. Jorgensen's book, *Lear's Self-Discovery*, states the main thesis of his study. Self-knowledge was a preoccupation of Shakespeare's contemporaries. Thus Lear's question "Who is it that can tell me who I am?" was the basis for a large body of writing published in the sixteenth and seventeenth centuries. In the beginning of the play, King Lear lacks self-knowledge; he is knowing but thoughtless. In the course of his affliction, suffering, and madness, he reaches self-knowledge and with it a recognition of man's frailty, of the necessary demands of bodily desire, and of problematical relationships to others. The King, unlike the villainous characters, learns that man requires three things: love, recognition by others, and an understanding of his humble and precarious condition in relation to Nature. These needs, Jorgensen argues, are equally valid today when many of us seek "identity" and fulfillment.

Maynard Mack begins his provocative and lucid *King Lear in Our Time* with a brief account of the play's stage history and intellectual context. He points out the successive failures of directors and critics who have distorted the play by concentrating on "motivating" interpretations of character. These efforts fail because *King Lear* will not submit to rationalization and unification. It remains irregular and enigmatic.

Mack explains this obdurate irregularity by arguing that Shakespeare's material came from medieval sources not amenable to modern psychological and rationalist preoccupations: archetypal stories, biblical injunctions, morality and miracle plays, and dream visions. Thus the characters and action of *King Lear* are both homiletic and dramatic, general and specific, at once abstract personification and concrete personality. Having such a pervasive multivalence, character and action will not fit into a rationalized scheme; instead they form a recurrent "pattern of the unexpected." Because such unexpectedness and disorder are the norm, what few relationships of order that exist are consequently portrayed as tenuous and irrational. The play thus relentlessly exposes the precariousness of human society, the necessity of its frail bonds, the interconnection of community and hierarchy, and the contrasts of an ideal with the real polity. *King Lear*, concludes Mack, is about the ties that bind us to each other and to an existence that is fundamentally tragic.

Perhaps the most unyielding and tough-minded interpretation of the play is that of S. L. Goldberg in his book, *An Essay on King Lear*. Recognizing with most critics that *King Lear* places great demands on our honesty of response and capacity to endure the almost unendurable injustice of the whole, Goldberg catalogues the play's several disquieting and unanswerable conditions: reversals of expectation, inevitable conflicts between public action and private emotion, collisions of personality, the need for love and the vulnerability consequent to that need. Urging us to *see* and then honestly acknowledge the grim facts of the human condition that the play reveals, he leads us to recognize and not evade our ambivalent responses to the action, our emotional and merciless wish for the evildoers to suffer punishing justice, our futile attempts to fashion comfortable interpretations for a play that steadily refuses to conform to any absolute or ultimate principles. Seen in this light, the drama of *King Lear* is almost unbearably ironic. Each of the characters is irrevocably trapped in contradictions and paradox. And the play as a whole posits an ironic "kinship between love of justice and love of cruelty," and a suspicion that the imposition of order at once diminishes the value of order. These dilemmas are brilliantly exposed in a knotty analysis of Act Three, most particularly the scenes of Lear on the heath.

Although the play delivers only "ambiguous silence" to the questions raised, it nevertheless puts forward such positive values as the necessity of tolerance, the recognition of vulnerability and weakness, and man's desire for love and affection. Yet King Lear, faced with a world in which these values are exceedingly rare, in which a divine purpose exists not at all, falls first into madness and finally into death.

In conclusion Goldberg reminds us that *King Lear* is not so much depressing as honest and intense. While moving us deeply, it also remains vitally open, thereby demanding from us a free and individual response to Shakespeare's most compelling tragic vision.

The summary paragraphs of the books mentioned above are necessarily compressed, mere sketches of the complex, learned, and detailed arguments put forward by the authors. It is hoped, however, that these introductory descriptions will encourage the reader to partake of the thoughts of those who keep bright the literary brilliance of *King Lear*. For a familiarity with the play leads not to contempt but illumination. As John Keats knew when he wrote his sonnet "On Sitting Down to Read *King Lear* Once Again," we uncover the springs of our being in this "fierce dispute / Betwixt damnation and impassioned clay," and find in it "our deep eternal theme!"

REFERENCES

Danby, John F., *Shakespeare's Doctrine of Nature, A Study of King Lear* (London: Faber and Faber Ltd., 1949).

Elton, William R., *King Lear and the Gods* (San Marino, California: The Huntington Library, 1966).

Fraser, Russell A., *Shakespeare's Poetics in Relation to King Lear* (London: Routledge and Kegan Paul, 1962).

Goldberg, S. L., *An Essay on King Lear* (London: Cambridge University Press, 1974).

Heilman, Robert B., *This Great Stage: Image and Structure in King Lear* (Baton Rouge: Louisiana State University Press, 1948).

Jorgensen, Paul A., *Lear's Self-Discovery* (Berkeley and Los Angeles: University of California Press, 1967).

Mack, Maynard, *King Lear in Our Time* (Berkeley and Los Angeles: University of California Press, 1965).

Rosenberg, Marvin, *The Masks of King Lear* (Berkeley and Los Angeles: University of California Press, 1972).